A Canoe Country Memoir

John C. Dailey

Sixty Years of Canoeing in the Quetico-Superior,
1956 – 2015

"So dat's the reason I drink tonight
   To de man of de Grand Nor' Wes',
For hees heart was young, and hees heart was light
   So Long as He's leevin' dere—
I'm proud of de sam' blood in my vein
   I'm a son of de Nort' Win wance again—
So we'll fill her up till de bottle's drain
   An' drink to de Voyageur."

–William Henry Drummond,

from the Voyageur and Other Poems

Also By John C. Dailey

AUTOBIOGRAPHICAL

a) Canoeing Around Hunter Island via Beaverhouse
b) October Surprise: Canoeing in the Wind, Ice and Snow of the BWCA
c) My First Canoe Trip – 1956
d) A Few Quetico Highlights
e) Six Canoe Country Men Who Influenced My Life
f) Pat and John's Fiftieth Wedding Anniversary Book

FICTION

Bennie the Woodchuck and the Gold Cup

POETRY

The Portage Trail and Other Journeys, Vol. 1 & 2

PRESENTATION

The American Chesterton Society Annual Meeting,
Mundelein, Illinois, August 1, 2014

"Chesterton at Notre Dame,
October-November 1930"

Copyright © 2022 by John C. Dailey

All rights reserved. No part of this book may be reproduced without the expressed written permission of John C. Dailey at joeseliga17@gmail.com

To obtain fine Giclee prints of the artwork in this book contact John C. Dailey at joeseliga17@gmail.com

Front cover image: Over the Beaver Dam by John Peyton.
Back cover image: John Dailey, 1959, Canoe Base Guide. Photo by Roy Conradi.
All interior images are by John Dailey unless otherwise noted.

Book design by Caroline Kiser Green

ISBN #: 978-0-9986044-7-3

Printed in the United States of America.

First Edition

This book is dedicated to Patricia Ann Dailey,
my wife of fifty-nine years and my best bowman.

Acknowledgements

This is the fifth book that I have had the privilege of working with Dr. James Veenstra who retired from medicine to pursue a full-time career as a fine art photographer and printer. Jim scanned all the photographs and paintings into a digital format and prepared them for transfer to Dropbox and converted the pdf files to word format. He provided invaluable help preparing the book for the designer and I am forever in his debt.

I am also fortunate that Caroline Kiser Green has once again undertaken the difficult task of transforming my words and pictures into a beautifully designed finished book. She is truly gifted. Thanks, Caroline.

Many thanks to Stuart Osthoff, publisher of the Boundary Waters Journal, for allowing me to incorporate the five articles I wrote for the Journal into this book. From the very first article I wrote for the Journal in 1988, Stu has been an inspiration to me.

Finally I am indebted to Kris and Doug Cameron from Hawk Ridge Art in Duluth who have given permission once again for me to reproduce pictures of my collection of John Peyton paintings.

Introduction

What you are about to read is a collection of stories about some of my experiences in the Quetico-Superior Country in northern Minnesota and southern Ontario over a period of 60 years from 1956, when I took my first canoe trip, until my last trip in 2015. Five of the stories previously appeared in *The Boundary Waters Journal*, published by Michele and Stuart Osthoff. They have been revised and expanded with more detail for this book. I hope all of the stories you are about to read convey my deep sense of respect and awe for this magnificent wilderness area. Going there for the first time in 1956 changed my life forever in ways I could never have anticipated. In addition, there are five poems interspersed throughout the stories from my book, *The Portage Trail and Other Journeys*. Chapter five is a collection of digitally captured John Peyton watercolor and oil paintings depicting various themes of the canoe country from my personal collection.

After that initial canoe trip in 1956 I literally fell in love with the canoe country. My friend Mark Spink helped me get a job at the Boy Scout Canoe Base on Moose Lake where I learned to be a canoe guide. When my guiding days ended in 1963, I spent the next 52 years canoeing in the Quetico-Superior with my family and friends until my last trip in 2015 which I took with my oldest grandson, Sean Michael Dailey. My only regret is that my days of canoe tripping are over but the memories linger on and I hope to share some of those with you.

When I decided to gather these stories together, the first thing that came to mind was how it all came to be. How could a teenager from Carrollton, a small rural town in central Illinois, become a wilderness canoe guide at the age of eighteen? I think the answer is due to the environment in which I grew up, my association with the Boy Scouts of America and my own personality.

I enjoyed a relatively carefree life as a teenager. I hung around with a bunch of guys my own age. We didn't have cell phones or computers or drugs or cars to deflect our lives. Girls were around too but they were not serious distractions. We rode our bikes everywhere. Our summers were filled with playing sports, roaming the woods, playing army with homemade rubber band guns, fishing and hunting, working odd jobs and the Boy Scouts.

Most of us were members of the local Boy Scout Troop led by Russel Wiles, a retired state policeman. Along with our weekly meetings. he kept us pretty busy working on merit badges and overnight campouts, and making plans to attend Camp Warren Levis, the Boy Scout Camp near Alton, Illinois. I spent a week there the first time in 1954. As a 14 year old First Class Scout, I earned a number of merit badges, including canoeing and rifle shooting, and started the process of earning other merit badges necessary to advance to Eagle Scout, my ultimate goal. The week I spent at Camp Warren Levis that year along with the other guys in my troop was the first time for most of us to attend a summer camp, and we had a great time. By the end of the week we were already talking about going back the following year and many of us did. I actually spent 2 weeks at the Camp in 1955 and earned enough merit badges to advance to Life Scout, and was chosen to be a member of the Order of the Arrow. I think it was those experiences at Camp Warren Levis that also prepared me for the things that were to happen in the summer of 1956.

Most of us had summer jobs in 1956. In addition to working around the house and mowing the yard with a push mower, young guys like me were needed by farmers to help pick up hay bales from the field, called bucking bales, and putting them in the barn. Besides earning $15.00 or so for a day's work, we were often invited to enjoy a big noonday meal with the farmer and his family. My second job was detasseling corn which started in late June and lasted for about a month. My 8 hour shift was from 4 AM until noon. It was hard, hot, sweaty work and only paid about $2.00 an hour. In addition to these summer jobs I was looking forward to going back to Camp Warren Levis in 1956 to hopefully finish up my merit badge work for Eagle Scout. That never happened.

My dad was a very busy family physician in Carrollton. When he could, he and I did a lot of things together: duck hunting, fishing, baseball games and roaming up and down the Mississippi River in our eighteen foot wooden John boat with a 25 hp Evinrude motor. My Uncle Jack, dad's older brother, had been trying to get dad to go on a Canadian canoe trip for sometime but dad kept putting it off because of his busy medical practice. In April of 1956 dad mentioned again that we'ed been invited by Uncle Jack to go on a canoe trip in July, and dad said we were going. I was excited about the prospect but then as the time approached for us to go I told dad that I wanted to stay home and continue working and be with my friends, and go to Scout Camp. My argument for staying home wasn't acceptable to dad and he insisted that I had to go with him. Looking back I can't believe I was so dense to want to give up an experience of a lifetime to stay home. Well the rest is history. Thanks, Dad.

John C. Dailey
January, 2022

N.B. The Fisher map, E-15, located inside the back cover of the book should help you to follow the various canoe trips described in the book. For those who are not used to using the map, locate Moose Lake at the end of the Moose Lake Road, which branches off the Fernberg Road in the BWCAW since most of the trips started there.

Table of Contents

Introduction 7

Chapter One...My First Canoe Trip – 1956 12

Chapter Two...The Charles L. Sommers Wilderness Canoe Base. 25
Part I: A Brief History of the Base to 2021 25
Part II: The Swamper Program, 1957 to 1961 30
Part III: A Canoe Base Guide, 1957 to 1961 34
Part IV: Epilogue. 38

Chapter Three...Canoeing Around Hunter Island via Beaverhouse 40

Chapter Four...Reflections on Canoeing in the Quetico Park.
   (A Few Quetico Highlights) 56
Trip 1: Looking for the Powell Lake Portage. 57
Trip 2: Journey to Poohbah Lake 63
Trip 3: Delahey Lake – 1958 68
Trip 4: Delahey Lake – 1961 73
Trip 5: Meadows Lake and the "Lost" Canoe 74

Chapter Five...A Collection of North Country Paintings by John Peyton 81

Chapter Six...Canoeing With My Wife. 114
Trip 1: McIntyre and Brent Lakes – 1964 114
Trip 2: Incident at Kawnipi Forks – 1968 119
Trip 3: Woodside Lake – 1970 121
Trip 4: Ottertrack Lake – 1982 122
Trip 5: That Man Lake – 1979 & 1984 124

Chapter Seven...Canoeing with Novices 127
Trip 1: A Windy Day on Basswood Lake – 1963. 127
Trip 2: BWCA Canoe Trip – 1971. 132
Trip 3: BWCA Canoe Trip – 1974. 134
Trip 4: BWCA Canoe Trip – 1979. 135

Chapter Eight...A Family Adventure – 1983. 140

Chapter Nine... October Surprise
Canoeing in the Wind, Ice and Snow of the BWCA – 2006. 151

Chapter Ten...Six Canoe Country Men Who Influenced My Life 162

Chapter Eleven...My Last Canoe Trip – 2015. 176

Chapter Twelve...Final Thoughts. 186

CHAPTER ONE

My First Canoe Trip*

When I was thirteen or fourteen, my dad occasionally talked about the two of us going on a Canadian canoe trip with my Uncle Jack, dad's older brother. He said the trip would start in Ely, Minnesota and would last for about ten days. Even though my mother was from Austin, Minnesota and I had two cousins who lived in Minneapolis, I had never heard of Ely so I didn't give it much thought at the time. Dad was a very busy medical doctor and it was difficult for him to take time off but he finally agreed that we would go on a trip that Uncle Jack was planning for July, 1956. I was sixteen at the time and was active in the Boy Scouts and had my canoeing merit badge. I was excited about the idea of the canoe trip but reluctant to go because I would have to quit my two summer jobs and cancel my plans to attend Scout camp. Strange isn't it how fate steps in when you least expect it and your life takes a whole new direction? That's what happened to me. Because my dad insisted I go with him on the canoe trip, my life changed forever on the border lakes of northern Minnesota and southern Ontario, the two and a half million acre wilderness paradise of glacial lakes and boreal forests situated on the southern edge of the Great Canadian Shield, "a large area of exposed Precambrian rocks that form the ancient core of the North American continent," also called the Laurentian Plateau. This is where my story begins.

Uncle Jack was an attorney who started canoeing in the Boundary Waters in the 1930's when he was still in college. He initially outfitted with Sig Olson at Border Lakes Outfitters on Fall Lake and then in the 1940's with Bill Rom at Canoe Country Outfitters. By the time of our 1956 canoe trip he was a veteran canoe tripper. Dad and I drove from our home in Carrollton, Illinois to Burlington, Iowa, where Uncle Jack and my two cousins lived. Our group consisted on Uncle Jack, my dad, me, age 16, my cousin Jim, Jack's son, age 20, and my cousin, Eddie, age 15, Jack's nephew. After a brief stop in Burlington we drove to Minneapolis where we stayed overnight and then on to Ely the next day. There were no super highways in 1956 but we managed to get to Cloquet, Minnesota, by about noon where we stopped for lunch in Pinehurst park where there was a large white bandshell that is still there. I just remember it was a long hot drive and we were relieved when we got to Ely in the late afternoon.

Because of Uncle Jack's friendship with Bill Rom, we outfitted with Canoe Country Outfitters on Sheridan Street. We met Bill and our guide, Mark Spink. My dad was apprehensive because this was his first canoe trip and he insisted that we take a guide along. Bill recommended Mark, a former guide at Sommers Canoe Base on Moose Lake and a veteran of the Army Air Corps in WW ll. Mark proved to be the perfect choice for the job, even acting as a buffer between dad and Uncle Jack at times when disagreements would arise on the trip.

The first thing we did after meeting Mark was to go over our gear and talk about where we wanted to go on the trip. Uncle Jack wanted to go

Lunch break in Cloquet, MN park. The band shell in the background is still there. Uncle Jack, John and cousin Eddie. July, 1956. Photo by Jim Dailey.

to McIntyre Lake in the Quetico Park. Mark mentioned that he had a favorite campsite on McIntyre so that worked out fine. Mark and Uncle Jack checked out the pack sacks which included the two heavy canvas wall tents that Uncle Jack insisted on taking. The food for our trip was supplied by Bernie Hutar who filled most of the food outfitting needs for Rom's at that time. Bernie owned Bernie's Food Market, a small grocery store on Central Avenue around the corner from the Forest Hotel, which was on Sheridan Street, the main street in Ely. Those were the days when there were no restrictions on cans and bottles in the canoe country. Mark tried to limit the canned goods but even so, the food packs were really heavy. All of the pack sacks we used were variations of the canvas Duluth pack. A favorite trick of the packers who prepared the packs for outgoing groups was to add a few rocks in the bottom of the packs "just for balance." Along with everything else we had twenty loaves of Master Bakery white bread; each loaf was compressed to about one-fourth its original size to fit in the pack sack.

After dinner at Vertine's Cafe which was located in the Forest Hotel (the Forest Hotel burned down in 1967. Vertine's Restaurant relocated a block away in the Piggly Wiggly store), we went back to the outfitters where we stayed in the Rom motel which was in a separate building behind the outfitting store. It rained all night but when we got up the next morning it was cool and sunny. We were all anxious to get started, especially Uncle Jack. Our packs and canoes were carried out to Fall Lake at Winton where Wilderness Outfitters had a large launch which hauled people and gear six miles up Fall Lake to the four-mile bus portage to Hoist Bay on Basswood Lake. The launch made two or three trips per day, depending on how many people were coming and going to Basswood Lodge, which was owned by Wilderness. When we got to Hoist Bay everything was transferred to another launch which took everyone to Basswood Lodge, a beautiful wilderness resort located a short distance away. Before leaving for the Lodge we visited the Paul Bunyan Shop, a neat little souvenir store which was located at the end of the bus portage on Hoist Bay. After a brief stop at the Lodge to drop off tourists and supplies, the launch took us about ten miles down the lake to Upper Basswood Falls where we unloaded everything and finally started our canoe trip.

One of the many memories I have of the canoe trip is that I was always hungry, especially for bread. We had plenty of food but as a growing teenager I just couldn't seem to get enough food. My cousin, Eddie, had the same problem. Anyway before we started the mile-long Horse Portage around Upper Basswood Falls, we had lunch which consisted of peanut butter sandwiches, cookies and Kool Aid. That was the first time I drank water right out of a lake without filtration. I have to admit that I have never varied from that practice in all the years I have been in the Canoe Country except to always get water from further out in the lake when we're in a campsite. We made it down the Basswood River in good shape and camped our first night on the Canadian side of Crooked Lake, just south of Moose Bay. One of the first things Mark did was to send Eddie and me to find some "beaver wood" for our campfire. That became one of our jobs throughout the trip. There was a bit of conflict that evening after supper. My dad insisted on washing the dishes in hot soapy water and rinsing them in hot water. Mark agreed with him but Uncle Jack didn't. He was used to just wiping off the plates and silverware and rinsing them in cold water. and only doing the soapy hot water routine midway through the trip. I am happy to say the my dad prevailed.

The next day, our second day, was a long one for me. We headed up to Moose Bay to Robinson Lake and then into Dart Lake and Cecil Lake where we finally stopped for lunch. There was a light rain and I was pretty tired and just wanted to stop for the day. We met a young couple who were on their honeymoon camped on Cecil. I remember thinking that was a strange place for a honeymoon but a few years later I changed my mind when I took my wife on her first canoe trip a few months after we were married. After our lunch of cheese and salami and lemonade, Mark encouraged us to keep moving as we just had a short paddle across Deer Lake and then a lift over portage into McIntyre Lake, our destination. He had a special campsite in mind for us and even promised fresh walleye for supper.

The campsite was indeed unique, hidden back in a little bay off the west side of the lake with a nice view of the sunset. After we unloaded our canoes, dad, my two cousins and I starting setting up camp while Mark and Uncle Jack rigged their lines with jigs and night crawlers and went to Mark's "secret" walleye hole. They caught a nice stringer of walleyes which we had for supper. Most of our camping equipment was very heavy by today's standards. Uncle Jack's tents were

McIntyre campsite, two wall tents, July 1956.

heavy canvas wall tents which we tied between two trees and then propped up the ends with poles cut from small trees which were usually left behind for the next campers. We didn't have light weight Thermarest sleeping pads which didn't come along until the 1970's. Instead we laid out our sleeping bags on the ground on top of a canvas ground cloth. (We didn't have air mattresses either.) Our seventeen foot aluminum canoes weighted about 75 pounds, and let's not forget the heavy food packs filled with canned goods. I managed to carry a canoe over a few short portages but it was a struggle, and I didn't learn how to flip a canoe onto my shoulders until a year later at the Canoe Base as noted in Chapter Two.

On day three, after a breakfast of bacon, pancakes and syrup, stewed fruit and hot cocoa, we all paddled down to the south end of our little "hidden" bay where there was another nice campsite nestled in a grove of white pines. It looked like a park. There were plenty of tent sites and a gigantic rock which provided protection from the wind. On the north end of the campsite there was a small waterfall where water from McIntyre poured into a beautiful little stream which

McIntyre campsite, cooking breakfast, Mark Spink and Uncle Jack in the red shirt.

eventually emptied into Robinson Lake to the south. Mark was interested in the stream because there were minnows in it and we spent some time seining for a few of them for fish bait. After catching enough walleyes for supper we headed back to our camp for lunch. Later that afternoon we heard someone calling for help from a campsite that was located about a mile south of us in the main part of the lake. Mark and I paddled there against a headwind. When we got there, the folks at the campsite told us there was no problem, they were just horsing around. Mark was not happy.

It was still windy on day four but Mark took my dad out to the main part of McIntyre to fish for lake trout. Dad caught three beautiful trout and kept one which he brought back for supper. Everyone was getting restless to move on to another lake so on day five we packed everything and moved to Conmee which Mark said was his favorite lake. We stopped for lunch on Airplane Island in Brent Lake and made it into Conmee in the late afternoon. Once we entered the main part of the lake Mark pointed to two small islands which he said was another walleye hole. After jigging for an hour we managed to hook about a dozen eating size walleyes which we planned to have for supper. This trip was the first time I had ever eaten fresh caught walleyes, cooked to perfection by Mark. Back home in Illinois we were used to eating catfish and buffalo. In fact we caught so many walleyes that we had enough left over to take with us when we left Conmee for our last camp in Sarah.

Our campsite in Conmee was located on the north side of the lake on a small island that Mark called Flat Rock Island. It was located just west of a larger island and very close to the long portage from Poohbah on the north side of the lake. Looking back at some of the pictures I took of the campsite, as you see illustrated on these pages, it would never have been my first choice as a place to camp. It had been used a lot as evidenced how beaten down the ground was although there were plenty of tent sites. Small Black Spruce were the main trees on the island with a few birch and aspen and Norway Red pines. It wasn't nearly as nice as our McIntyre campsite and there was no place to swim. The water along the shoreline was very shallow and it had a dark color, and it looked like the birch trees on the south side of the lake all suffered from some type of blight.

The big wall tent on the Flat Rock Island campsite.

Conmee Lake, Flat Rock Island campsite. Dad is doing surgery on Mark's ingrown toenail who is sitting on a large rock to the left in the picture.

One of the many memories I have of our trip was my dad doing surgery on Mark. Day six, our first full day on Conmee, was bright and sunny. After a breakfast of pancakes and bacon, Mark announced that he was having a lot of pain in the big toe of his left foot. Apparently it had been bothering him for some time but he kept ignoring it. Dad examined him and found he had an infected ingrown toenail. Dad had brought along a minor surgery and first aid kit which had not yet been put to use. He had Mark sit on a big rock that was in the middle of the campsite and removed the ingrown nail, using a local anesthetic and a heavy scissors. That resolved the problem. I think Dad also gave him some penicillin which he had also brought along.

My most memorable recollection of Conmee happened on day seven, just to the east of Flat Rock Island in a small weedy bay where I caught my big fish. When I woke up that morning, it was overcast and a light rain was falling. Mark had put up the rain fly over the fireplace the night before. When I got out of the tent he had oatmeal with raisins cooking. He pointed out how one can tell when it was ready, when the oatmeal makes a popping or "plucking" sound. My cousin Eddie followed me out of the tent and we both had some oatmeal with brown sugar and butter and a few slices of bacon. We were anxious to go fishing so after breakfast we loaded our fishing tackle into a canoe. Mark told us we should go over towards the island just east of us and start trolling. We were using silver spoons and night crawlers. We gradually worked our way into a small weedy bay and almost immediately got snagged on the weeds. We then tried casting with surface lures but were unsuccessful so we started trolling again slowly with daredevil spoons. I was paddling in the stern and had let out a lot of line. When I started to reel it in I felt a sudden tugging on the line. I kept reeling but there was still a lot of resistance and I thought I had another snag. I stopped paddling and I kept trying to get the line in without losing the spoon. The tugging continued and I started to wonder if maybe I had a fish rather than a snag. I was using a Shakespeare spinning rod and reel that dad had given to me along with ten-pound mono line and a steel leader. I didn't want to pull too hard for fear the line might break. I set the drag and kept reeling, and after what seemed like forever, a giant Northern Pike covered with weeds surfaced alongside the canoe then immediately dove under the canoe, taking line out again and pulling the rod tip into the water. This occurred three or four more times before the fish just stayed on the surface next to the canoe. Eddie and I were both surprised beyond belief at the size of the fish, yelling and screaming with excitement. We didn't have a landing net but somehow we got the fish into the canoe without swamping. Once the fish was secured we quickly paddled the short distance back to our camp.

Everyone shared our excitement and I had my picture taken holding the fish and then Mark gave me the bad news. I wanted to keep the fish but Mark said we had to release it. We didn't have a scale but he thought it weighed about twenty-five pounds and was about three feet long. Looking back I know it was the right thing to release it but it was hard for me to do at the time. Anyway, I carefully put the fish back in the water and massaged its back like Mark showed me. Pretty soon it started moving its tail and then is swam off into the dark water. I've caught bigger fish since then (a sailfish off the coast of North Carolina) but I still get goose bumps when I think about that fish. I even had a dream one night that the fish got away.

John holding his big fish.

We left Flat Rock Island the next day and moved down to Sarah Lake where we had a beautiful campsite on Bear Island. We all swam in the crystal clear water of Sarah and had our last walleye dinner with the extra fish we had caught in Conmee. The next day, the last day of our trip, we went through Side and Isabella Lakes and then the beaver stream to North Bay where we met the launch from Basswood Lodge in the late afternoon. We stopped at the Lodge for awhile and then headed back to the four-mile bus portage that took us from Hoist Bay to Fall Lake and then one more launch ride down Fall Lake to Winton.

That was the only time I was on a canoe trip with Uncle Jack and my two cousins. Uncle Jack made a few more canoe trips over the years with other groups but I'm not sure if my cousins ever did. Years later I spent some time with him talking about his experiences in the canoe country, the last time just a month before he died in nineteen seventy-six. Dad and I took three more trips together and even made it back to McIntyre and Conmee. Our last trip together was when I graduated from medical school in nineteen sixty-six. He died in nineteen seventy-eight. Mark and I remained friends for many years. He was a very special kind of guy who loved the canoe country. The last time I saw him was in nineteen eighty-nine when he was about to retire from the University of Western Michigan in Kalamazoo where he was an award-winning film producer and professor of media services. Mark died in 2012.

I could never have anticipated the effect being in the canoe country had on me. Our family had vacationed at the Sha Sha Resort on Rainy Lake when I was twelve. But a wilderness canoe trip is something entirely different than fishing with a boat and motor on Rainy Lake. I was captivated by the idea that we passed into a different world when we left civilization behind at the first portage, depending on ourselves to survive the rigors of the wilderness. Mark's stories about the history of the canoe country, especially the stories about the French Voyageurs, added to the mystique of the experience. In fact I was so enamored with the whole concept of wilderness canoeing and camping that I told Mark I wanted to be a guide like him and asked if he could help me in that respect. He said the best place to start would be at the Boy Scout Canoe Base on Moose Lake and he promised to write a letter of recommendation, which he did, and changed the course of my life.

* This story first appeared in the Winter 2018 issue of *the Boundary Waters Journal*.
  It has been slightly revised and expanded for this book.

A Quetico Day

The surface of Conmee Lake was like a mirror,
Reflecting the outline of our canoe.
The fading light a reminder that sundown was near.
The haunting, mournful loon-song added to
The sense that peace and solitude were here.

Quietly, slowly we dipped our blades
Into the water and began to glide across
The lake. The canvas-covered hull was made
To slide easily on the smooth and glossy
Surface. All is still as daylight fades.

We landed the canoe by the rocky outcrop
Where we had earlier set up camp.
The air was cooler now so we stopped
To build up our fire. We were damp
From paddling and an unexpected shower of raindrops.

At first light we loaded the canoe with our packs,
The cargo evenly spaced 'tween bow and stern.
Paddling near shore, the wind at our backs,
We moved quickly at first then started to turn
Toward a distant point, always staying on track.

As paddlers we work as one
To propel the craft across the lake.
Both pulling back water, we began to hum
A voyageur's song, "A la claire fontaine...," *
And bathe in the warmth of the morning sun.

Our Seliga was made for this kind of trip,
Crafted with care of canvas and wood.
A solid vessel designed to slip
With ease in bad weather and good,
Through rough seas and calm, a seaworthy ship.

We soon reached the portage back in the bay.
While our canoe floated next to the land
The packs were unloaded and placed safely away
On the shore. Picking up our gear, the canoe tied to a stand
Of alder brush, we started down the trail on our way.

We hustled back for the canoe
And the rest of the gear. I flipped
It on to my shoulders. It wasn't too
Heavy, about eighty-five pounds. I slipped
On some rocks but carried it all the way through.

And so we moved on for the rest of the day,
From portage to portage and from lake
To lake, stopping to rest now and then and to say
A prayer that no one would take
The campsite on Keefer where we planned to stay.

* "At the clear running fountain…"

CHAPTER TWO

The Charles L. Sommers Wilderness Canoe Base

PART ONE: A BRIEF HISTORY OF THE BASE UP TO 1966.

We were known as "Charlie's Boys." A least that's the way most of us affectionately referred to ourselves. "Charlie's Boys" were the Canoe Base guides and other associated members of the staff of the Charles L. Sommers Canoe Base in 1957 when I started working there. All of the guides and Base staff were men. The only females that I recall being there were the Base Director Cliff Hanson's wife and his daughter.

The Canoe Base is owned and operated by the Boy Scouts of America. It is located on Moose Lake on the edge of the Boundary Waters Canoe Area Wilderness (BWCAW) about twenty-five miles from Ely, Minnesota. It was officially opened in May, 1942, and named in honor of Mr. Charles L. Sommers, a business man from St. Paul who was long associated with the scouting program. The history of the Canoe Base up to 1966 was recorded in a book by the same name, *Canoe Base,* written by Mr. George D. Hedrick and published by the Boy Scouts of America. Much of the information in Part One about the early history of the Canoe Base is based on Mr. Hedrick's book.[1]

Mr. Carl S. Chase actually originated the idea of organized Boy Scout canoe trips in 1923. The first few trips into the border lakes were sponsored by the Virginia, Minnesota Scout Council with Mr. Chase acting as the adult leader. It was somewhat fortuitous that the Region Ten Scout Executive from St. Paul, H.F. Pote, visited the Virginia area in the winter of 1925 and met with Mr. Chase. After learning about the success of the canoe trips, he and Chase decided to develop the canoe trip concept into a Regional project. The necessary financial backing was secured from two Twin City canoeing enthusiasts, Mr. Charles L. Sommers and Mr. F.A. Bean. And so it was that in the summer of 1926, the Region Ten Wilderness Canoe Trails Program began to operate out of Fall Lake at Winton, Minnesota, with Carl Chase as the director. From 1925 through 1932 a total of 446 scouts participated in the project.

In 1933 the Canoe Trails Program was moved to the Canadian Border Lodge at the south end of Moose Lake. Moose Lake provided greater proximity and more access to routes into the border lakes than were available at Fall Lake. In 1936 another move was made, this time to Hibbard's Resort, further east on Moose Lake. No reason was given for this although Mr. Hibbard did build a bunkhouse for the scouts which would accommodate up to forty people.

Mr. Hedrick noted that the basic theme of the Canoe Trails Program was "to provide a high adventure camping experience in keeping with the purposes and ideals of the Boy Scouts of America for the older boys of the movement." In the early days (1932) this meant that to participate, a scout had to be at least fifteen years old and should have attained a minimum rank of First Class. This concept prevailed in later years and if anything, the requirements became even more strict. In addition, one of the original goals of the Canoe Base was to provide access to the canoe country at a reasonable price. In 1957, for example, the cost for the entire outfitting including two nights lodging and four meals at the Base and the Canoe Base guide, was $37.00 per person.

With each passing year the popularity of the Canoe Trails Program increased. From 1933 to 1939 the number of scout participating in the program totaled 739, almost double from the previous eight years. Along with this increased enthusiasm, Carl Chase and the staff from the Region Ten office in St. Paul realized that a permanent base of operations needed to be established. Further impetus to this desire came from none other that Mr. F. A. Bean. He reportedly felt that the establishment of a permanent canoe base would be a good way to honor he close friend and long-time associate, Charles L. Sommers.

In 1940 a search committee was formed to start looking around the area for land upon which to build a permanent base. A number of locations were inspected, including the Lac La Croix area, the Nina Moose River, and the Gunflint region. However, none of those sites were found to be satisfactory. The committee then made contact with Mr. William Trigg, the U.S. District Forester in Ely. Trigg met with the group and showed them a small parcel of land which the Forest Service owned on the southeast shore of Moose Lake, about a mile beyond the end of the Moose Lake Road. To everyone's delight, the site met all of the qualifications. On September 23, 1941, a special use permit was issued by the Forest Service for the Boy Scouts of America to build a canoe base there. (I had the honor to meet Mr. Trigg in 1969 when I was looking for property on Burntside lake. His son, Bill, actually handled the sale.)

The first two buildings at the Base were constructed during the winter of 1941. They were made from pine logs which had been harvested from a blowdown on the Echo Trail and transported by truck to the Base. Seven Finnish craftsmen were hired to do the work. Using only hand tools, they constructed two log structures, the story and a half, fifty-six by thirty-six foot main lodge and a smaller combination wash house and latrine. These buildings still stand today as a testament to their craftsmanship. A number of buildings have been added up through 1967 when Mr. Hedrick wrote his monograph including the F.A. Bean Bay Post, the guide's quarters or Tepee and a new mess hall. These were present when I worked at the Base from 1957 to 1961. Since then many new buildings have been added, and the old Tepee and Bay Post have been replaced with new structures.

The Teepee, the guide quarters, Sommers Canoe Base, 1957. Staff members would meet there and read and relax. There were showers on the lower level. After the paddles for the crews were painted red on the tip and branded with an "X", they were hung up on the railing to dry.

From its beginning in 1942 and up to the present time, the Charles L. Sommers Wilderness Canoe Base has remained an important fixture in the scouting program. The Boy Scouts of America were originally organized into twelve regions. The Canoe Base was in Region Ten which was headquartered in St Paul. In 1972 that all changed and the Regional offices were closed and the Canoe Base came under the direct control of the National Office of the Boy Scouts of America which is located in Irving, Texas.[2] The Base was renamed the Charles L. Sommers Northern Tier High Adventure Base under the leadership of the new base director, former guide, Sandy Bridges. Winter camping trips, termed *Okpic*, started in the early 1970's and have been an important adjunct to the summer program. Two Canadian outpost Bases were also opened, the Donald Rogert Canoe Base near Atikokan, Ontario, and the Northern Expeditions Canoe Base near Bissett, Manitoba. These resulted from the desire to explore new wilderness areas and to adapt to the relative shortage of camping permits available for the Quetico Park and the BWCAW.[3]

Display of Patches from the original twelve regions of the Boy Scouts of America. Photo by Jim Veenstra.

A number of other changes have taken place since my last year as a canoe guide at the Base in 1961. The canoe guides are no longer referred to as "guides." Because of new regulations, everyone who guides commercially in the BWCAW, such as would be the case if you are guiding scouts from the Canoe Base, is required to have a license issued by the US Forest Service. If you are guiding commercially in the Quetico Park or elsewhere in Canada, you are required to have a work permit issued through Canadian Immigration. In order to avoid these bureaucratic expenses, the Canoe Base guides are now referred to as "interpreters."[4][5][6] The size of the crews that are outfitted at Sommers Canoe Base are limited to nine people which includes the interpreter. This is because in the 1970's the Forest Service issued a ruling that no more than ten people could camp at a designated camp site. (The Ten-Party Rule: this was also the rule in the Quetico.) Two members of the group should be 21 or older. When I was guiding at the Base I sometimes had as many as 18 in the group though we tried to keep the size of the group to 12 which included the guide. The total number of scouts that were outfitted from 1954 through 1966 averaged about 2370 per summer.[7] We used Seliga and Old Town wooden canoes along with Grumman aluminum canoes. Now the light-weight kevlar canoes and the 17 foot Alumacraft are the canoes of choice. The number of scouts that are outfitted at Sommers Canoe Base now averages about 4500 from June through August. The summer of 2021 will probably see about 5500 scouts outfitted. The cost for outfitting at the Moose Lake Base in 2021 is $800.00 per day for a crew which includes the interpreter. Thus a seven day canoe trip would cost $5600.00. The cost for trips through the Atikokan and the Manitoba Bases are more.[8]

The changes listed above are not surprising in light of how so many things have changed in today's world. When I bought my first VW Beetle in 1962 it cost about $1800.00. The 2019 VW Beetle base price was about $20,000.00. And so the present day fee of going on a guided canoe trip with all the new light weight equipment and added peripheral expenses is understandable but unfortunate. The other major change which has happened at the Canoe Base is "Diversity" with male and female "interpreters," and crews consisting of all males or all females or a mix of males and females.[9] I think it's great that women are playing an important role as guides at the Base. Both of my daughters and my wife are veteran canoe trippers in the Quetico and the BWCA, though I don't think my daughters ever aspired to be guides.

PART TWO: THE SWAMPER PROGRAM: 1957-1961

Standing next to my suitcase and pack, I waved goodbye to my folks as they drove away from the Canoe Base parking lot. The dust was starting to settle on the gravel road as they headed back to Ely and home to Illinois. I picked up my suitcase and pack and started heading up the trail to the Canoe Base Office. It was a hot summer afternoon in July, 1957 and I was about to begin a whole new endeavor. Mark Spink, the guide on my first canoe trip in 1956 and a veteran Canoe Base Guide, had written a letter to the Region Ten office in St. Paul recommending me for a job at the Canoe Base. Because I didn't have any guiding experience, I was invited to come to the Base to work as a Swamper, a guide in training. One of the prerequisites for the program was you had to be active in Scouting which I was, having attained the rank of Life Scout and was on my way to Eagle status. I was excited about being at the Base but was also apprehensive. I had never been so far away from home by myself and I wasn't sure if I would be able to meet the challenge.

The first person I met was Cliff Hanson, the Base Director. He immediately allayed some of my anxiety as he showed me around the Base (this was Cliff's first year as Base Director. He proved to be the right man for the job and was always available to listen to our problems and provide advice.) He mentioned that everyone who was at the Base shared a common sentiment, a love for adventure and for the Quetico-Superior Country. As we were talking, Henry Bradelich, the assistant Base Director, and Dave Zieganhagan, the Guide Chief, joined us. They mentioned there were two other swampers who would be in training with me, Jay Poole from Meadville, Pennsylvania, and Barry Bain from Del Rio, Texas. Dave reminded me that since the swamper program only lasted for four weeks, I would have to work hard to make a good impression. While it was a nonpaying job, room and board were provided along with a canoe trip at the end of the Base training session with a senior guide and a crew of scouts.

During the first two weeks or so the swamper worked at the base primarily under the direction of Henry and to a lesser extent, with Dave. Their job was to work the heck of the swampers and at the same time try to determine if they possessed the leadership qualities required to be a guide. The second half of the program consisted of going on a nine-day canoe trip into the Quetico Provincial Park with a senior guide and crew. Each group of scouts was called a "crew," ideally consisting of ten scouts, one adult leader and the guide from the Base.

In spite of our comprehensive orientation I was still unprepared for the amount of "hard labor" which filled our first days at the Base. We worked as painters, carpenters, road builders and handymen. That was in addition to doing KP duty at the mess hall. Thanks to Henry, all the work got done. He had a knack for finding jobs when there didn't seem to be anything left to do. In the evenings after our work was done, Henry would sit down with us in the Lodge and talk about the history of the canoe country, and inspire us with stories of the exploits of some of the previous guides. We often spent time talking with the present guides trying to absorb some of their experiences.

At the start of our training, Dave Zieganhagan took us down to the waterfront where the canoes were stored and told us we should pick out a canoe that we would use on our upcoming canoe trip. In 1957 all of the canoes at the Base were 17 foot wooden canoes, either Old Towns, made in Old Town Maine, or Seligas, which were made in Ely by Joe Seliga. The Old Town bottoms were covered with canvas and the Seligas had fiberglass bottoms They were heavy by today's standards, 80 to 100 pounds for the Old Towns and 70 to 80 pounds for the Seligas. Wooden canoes were a tradition at the Base. Part of a guide's reputation was determined by the type of canoe he used and how much weight he could carry over the portages. Aluminum canoes were of course used by the commercial outfitters but there was a definite distaste among the guides for the "tin cans," as we called them. We also had to learn how to "flip" a canoe; that is, we had to learn how to get the canoe into carrying position on our shoulders single-handedly, whether it was in the water on on the ground. The technique once mastered seems rather easy but for a while I was not sure that I could do it. Just before leaving from home in Illinois to come to the Canoe Base, I had lifted something and had immediate pain in my back. The pain was still present when I started the swamper program and when I first attempted to flip the canoe I had chosen, a 90 pound Old Town, I really had a lot of back pain and I just couldn't do it. I figured that was the end for me. A guy who can't flip his canoe is not going to be a guide. I think I took some aspirin and decided to try again the next day. When I did, I heard a crunching sound in my back and the pain was gone, never to return until about 30 years later when I underwent two back surgeries for a lumbar disc condition.

In essence, the person who is to carry the canoe stands midway between the bow and the stern where the carrying yoke is located. Grasping the near gunnel

John Dailey in his Old Town Canoe, Moose Lake, 1958. Photographer unknown.

with both hands, the canoe is lifted up onto the thighs while at the same time bending the knees slightly and leaning backwards. If you are on the left side of the canoe, you reach with the left hand for the opposite gunnel while at the same time placing the right arm under the near side of the canoe. By pushing and lifting with the right arm and pulling with the left arm and standing up from the bent-knee position, the canoe is rolled or flipped onto the shoulders with the pads of the yoke coming to rest on either side of your neck. If you flip the canoe from the right side, the hand and arm movements are just reversed. Good footing and coordination are essential and of course, lots of practice and determination.

Dave finally gave me the news that I had been waiting for, a canoe trip with a senior guide. I was assigned to a Ron Walls, a guide who was just a year older than me, but seemed older. Physically he matched some of the historical descriptions that we have of the French Voyageurs: tough, not too tall and very resourceful. He was also a good leader. Our crew of scouts was from Cleveland, Ohio. The trip took us into the heart of the Quetico Park, and as I think back on

that trip I can still see all of us in our canoes as we paddled against the wind up Agnes and on into Kawnipi. After a layover day in Kawnipi, we paddled all day in a torrential downpour, finally making camp in Russel Lake. From there we moved on to the west end of Sturgeon Lake, then down the Maligne River, across the Tanner portage into the Darky River and then into Darky Lake. The next day we had a strong tailwind from the west and used our tarps for sails as the wind pushed our canoes across Brent and McIntyre to the Sarah Lake portage. After spending the night in Sarah, the following day we set up camp on the Bayley Bay sandy beach and spent the day cleaning up discarded tin cans that were piled up on the beach by sinking them in the lake. We sunk about six canoe loads of cans. (This was the Canadian Ranger recommended disposal method for tin cans.) On the last day of our trip we paddled across Bayley Bay to Prairie Portage and back to Moose Lake and the Base.

Ron Walls on my swamper trip talking to a crew member, Kawnipi Lake, July 1957.

The trip took eight and one half days. Not only was it physically demanding but fighting the natural elements and my own lack of experience at the beginning seemed to be an insurmountable task. There were fourteen in our group and that required five heavy wooden canoes. We had four food packs that weighed about 100 pounds each at the beginning of our trip. When you add to that the pack of tents and the kettle pack along with five personal packs you can see that our canoes were loaded to the limit. None of the equipment we took was up to today's light-weight standards. And yet when we finished the trip we all enjoyed a real sense of satisfaction. A great challenge had been met and we had overcome it. We were no longer just scouts: we were voyageurs. We had stepped back in time for a few days and lived the life of the Ojibway and the fur trader and yes, even Paul Bunyan. One of the things I learned on the trip was how to drink water from the lake as you're paddling along and you don't have a cup. You simply hold your wet paddle overhead and drink the water as it drips off the blade. It works pretty well but it's not too sanitary.

PART THREE: A CANOE BASE GUIDE: 1957- 1961

Exhausted but exhilarated, the last Wind Lake portage behind us, our paddles moved rapidly beside the canoe as we raced across Moose Lake toward the Canoe Base. Another canoe trip, my last for the year, was nearly over. Glancing back, I spied a canoe about to pass on our port side. I yelled to my bowman to switch sides and paddle harder, a technique I often used to put fresh muscle energy into our strokes. Like an arrow, our canoe shot forward with a final burst of energy; and then we were home. A couple of guides were standing by the waterfront where we landed and shouted, "HOLRY" as we landed. That was the traditional way of greeting another group of scouts. The term comes from the whole wheat crackers that each crew carried. The packs and other gear were quickly unloaded onto the Base docking area as we stood in the water next to the canoes to protect them from bumping into the dock until we could lift them out of the water and store them on the nearby canoe racks.

All of the other crews from our group who started nine days ago had been at the Base for at least an hour according to Roy Conradi, the Base photographer, who watched us unload. Roy usually hung around the waterfront when crews came in, hoping to take orders for pictures of the returning "voyageurs." Roy did nice

work and I occasionally had him take my picture in my guide paraphernalia for the folks back home.

Starting up the hill toward the F.A. Bean Bay Post, I hesitated momentarily for one last look across the lake at the birch and aspen trees on the opposite shore which were beginning to take on the golden hue of autumn. Even though the late August air was unseasonably crisp, I noticed that I was still perspiring from the vigorous paddling. Moving on up the trail, I checked in my gear with the quartermaster, "Black Jack" Putman. As usual he was in a cantankerous mood, anxious to get to the mess hall and upset that my crews always got in so late. Hailing from Texas City, Texas, Jack was quite a character who didn't mince words but was more bark than bite. I think he got his nickname from his slicked-back, coal-back hair and beard and the fact that he resembled one of the pirates from "Treasure Island." My crews were usually the last ones to come in at the end of the trip because I always camped either on Basswood Lake or Wind Lake on our last night, rather than close to the Base on New Found or Sucker Lake. One reason was if there was a shortage of guides for the new groups starting out the guide chief, Dave Zieganhagan, would go out looking for a guide for a crew who was to come in the next day and bring him back to the Base to take the new crew, leaving his old crew to fend for themselves. Also the campsites in New Found and Sucker weren't very nice.

Tradition was an important part of life at the Canoe Base. One tradition was that each crew took a sauna and shower after the canoe trip. Sitting in the hot steamy sauna followed by a cool shower did wonders to loosen the accumulated grit and grime from one's pores. Sandy Bridges and his crew were just finishing up when my group got to the sauna. Sandy was one of the new guides who had started in 1959, my second year guiding at the Base. Sandy was from Little Rock, Arkansas, and was very popular with the guides and the crews. He had a distinctive southern accent and a quiet and unassuming demeanor which was one of his trademarks. He had an outstanding career as a guide and later became the Base Director, a position he held until his untimely death from lung cancer in 1997.

Another Tradition was the turkey dinner with all the trimmings which was served to the crews at the end of their trip. That was quite a treat after eating trail food for nine days. I suppose the most important tradition was the final gathering of everyone at dusk in the Main Lodge for our last campfire together. Awards were given out and then, in typical scouting fashion, we entertained each other with

skits and swapped stories about what happened on our various canoe trips. The evening closed with a prayer asking that "...the Great Master of all good scouts be with us until we meet again..." All the crews left the next morning after breakfast and preparations were begun for the new crews that would be coming in that afternoon. After each trip we were supposed to get a day off to take care of personal needs and hopefully have a chance to go into Ely to Vertin's Restaurant for a hamburger and maybe have a beer at Dee's Bar or the Jugoslav National Home Bar located above the JC Penny Store (I never had my ID checked).

My second year of guiding at the Canoe Base, 1959, finally came to an end and I was ready to return to college. It had been a long season with eight canoe trips and more than 70 days and nights camped in the Quetico-Superior Country. I didn't make it back for the 1960 season, attending summer school at the

Sommers Canoe Base Staff, June, 1959. John Dailey is standing in line 4, 4th from the left, with his arms folded Photo by Roy Conradi, Base Photographer.

University of Wyoming instead, but I did make it back for a final season of guiding at the Base during the summer of 1961 and then spent the summers of 1962 and 1963 guiding for the commercial outfitters in Ely.

My experiences at the Canoe Base taught me more than I ever could have imagined possible. I remember reminiscing with the other guides about how fortunate we were to be getting paid to do the things we would have been happy to do for nothing. Even though our salaries didn't amount to much by today's standards, each of us who worked at the Base at that time considered ourselves very fortunate indeed. All of us owe a debt of gratitude to the men of vision like Carl Chase, Charles L Sommers, F.A. Bean and of course H.F. Pote, all of whom helped bring the Canoe Base into existence through their efforts. There is so much one could say about the Base that it is difficult to know just where to begin and where to end. Perhaps the following words quoted by George Hedrick from the log of M.L. Johnson in 1943 says it all:

Sommers Canoe Base Christmas Card, December 1959. Photo by Roy Conradi, Base Photographer.

> *"It is good to be back at the Base. Civilized clothing feels stuffy - what possible good is a tie to a man anyway? Why should my billfold have dozens of required identifications, etc.? The lakes ask me for no name - only that I be a man."* (10)

PART FOUR: EPILOGUE

We are all voyageurs in this world, as we move along and travel the road of life. As guides at the Canoe Base we took on the persona of the French Voyageur. We started out as *mangeur de lard* ("pork eater"), or novice. Some of us became *hivernants* ("winterers"), experienced voyageurs. Then some advanced to become *bourgeois* ("propriaters"), or the one in charge, like my friend Sandy Bridges.[11]

Most of us who guided crews at the Base with Sandy, have set aside our paddles and packs to pursue other interests but I know we all feel that restless urge to move on down the lake when we hear the loon calling or smell the sent of the balsam pine wafting on the breeze.

Grace Lee Nute in her book, *The Voyageur*, has recorded an interesting comment by an older voyageur from the 1855 Journal of Alexander Ross: "...I'm past seventy years; been forty-two years in this country, for twenty-four I was a light canoeman. I required little sleep, no portage was too long for me. My end of the canoe never touched the ground till I saw the end of it. Fifty songs a day were nothing for me, I could carry, paddle, walk, and sing with any man I ever saw. I saved the lives of ten Bourgeois, and was always the favourite, because when others stopped to carry at a bad step, and lost time, I pushed on – over rapids, over cascades, over chutes; all were the same to me. No water, no weather ever stopped the paddle or the song. I had twelve wives in the country and once possessed fifty horses and six running dogs...I wanted for nothing and I spent all my earnings in the enjoyment of pleasure. Five hundred pounds, twice told, have passed through my hands; although now I have not a spare shirt on my back, nor a penny to buy one. Yet, were I young again, I should glory in commencing the same career again."[12]

REFERENCES:

1. George D Hedrick, *Canoe Base*, Boy Scouts of America, Region Ten, St. Paul, Minnesota, 1967

2. George D. Hedrick, Personal Letter, 5/27/1987

3. Canoe Bases of Northern Tier National High Adventure Bases, Charles L. Sommers Alumni Association, Inc., Box 425, Ely, Minnesota 55731

4. IBID, "Charlies Guides," Interpreters

5. Personal Communication, Charles L. Sommers Base Staff, June & August, 2021

6. Gene Felton, *A Diamond in the North,* North Star Publisher, 1998, p 74

7. George D. Hedrick, p. 62

8. Personal Communication, Charles L. Sommers Base Staff, June & August, 2021

9. IBID

10. George D. Hedrick, p. 61

11. Grace Lee Nute, *The Voyageur*, Minnesota Historical Society, St. Paul, Minnesota, 1955, p 5

12. IBID, pp 207-208

CHAPTER THREE

Canoeing Around Hunter Island via Beaverhouse *

Hunter Island is a land mass shaped like a rhombus. It comprises the lower two-thirds of the Quetico Provincial Park which is located along the Minnesota border opposite the Boundary Waters Canoe Area Wilderness (BWCAW.) It is not an island in the way we think of an island, like the island of Hawaii or Staten Island in New York. But in the strict sense it is an island for it is surrounded by the waters of 18 lakes and rivers. Starting at Prairie Portage in the BWCAW and going in a clockwise direction, the major lakes and rivers that encircle Hunter Island include Basswood Lake and the Basswood River, Crooked Lake, Iron Lake, Lac La Croix, the Maligne River, Sturgeon, Russell, Chatterton, Keats, Shelley and Kawnipi Lakes, the Falls Chain, Saganagons, Saganaga, Ottertrack, Knife and Birch Lakes. The distance around Hunter island following the aforementioned

Outline of Hunter Island on the Fisher Map, E-15 which is with the book. Hunter Island is outlined in red and the additional route through Beaverhouse is outlined in black. Photo by Jim Veenstra.

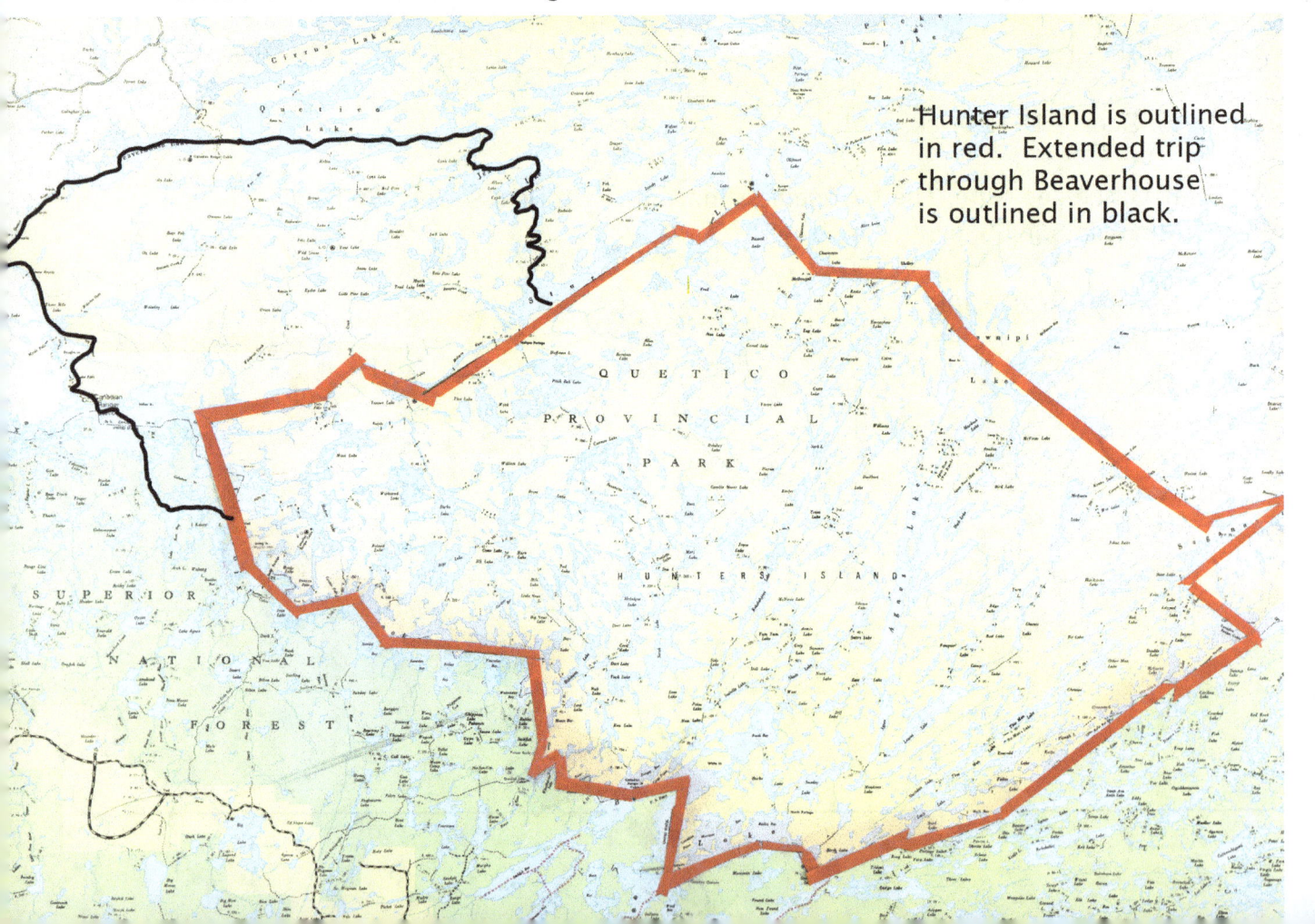

route is about 160 miles. If the route is extended by going north from Sturgeon into Jean, Quetico and Beaverhouse Lakes and then back to Lac La Croix via the Quetico and Namakan Rivers, that adds an additional 60 miles or so for a total of about 220 miles.

In 1958, when I first started working as a guide at the Charles L. Sommers Canoe Base, located on Moose Lake, I often listened to the veteran guides as they talked about their experiences, particularly their stories about the more difficult canoe trips in the Quetico Park. The Hunter Island route was considered a real challenge because Canoe Base trips were limited to eight and half days and to complete the 160 mile trip one would have to average about 19 miles per day. Few if any guides took their crews on such long trips for it meant paddling and portaging every day with little or no time for fishing or relaxation. I suppose I would never have made the Hunter Island trip if it were not for a number of things that happened that first week in July, 1958.

To begin with, I had just returned from my second guiding trip as a full-fledged guide, and I was in a rather dejected state of mind. The trip had been both physically and emotionally demanding, primarily because I had not gotten along well with the crew of scouts or their adult leader. The crew was from Texas and most of the guys were my age or older than me and they had a hard time accepting the fact that I was in charge. Their adult leader was also resistant to my authority. They were careless with the equipment, such as dragging the canoes on the ground on the portages, which added to my frustration with them. The crew actually threatened me with bodily harm at one point. The trip we took was difficult and I think that added to their unhappiness. I took them on the same trip I had taken the year before with Ron Walls when I was a swamper, which is described in Chapter Two of this book. I was also probably partly to blame for not being more accommodating. When we got back to the Base I received a poor evaluation from them which I kind of expected, but my self-esteem and confidence levels were at a low ebb. I actually considered quitting my work as a guide and leaving the Canoe Base.

The next day after that trip, I had a long talk with Cliff Hanson, the Base Director. Cliff was a real gentleman and he took a personal interest in the staff that worked at the Base. He encouraged me to forget about the trip and look to the future, not the past. He reminded me that life must go on in spite of our mistakes

and unhappy experiences. He urged my not to give up on myself but to keep going, following the philosophy of the Scouting Program and the Canoe Base. His inspiring words have stayed with me through the years.

Henry Bradelich, the assistant Base Director, was also very understanding and supportive. He was a former guide and he understood the problems we encountered in the woods. During the off season, Henry taught school in Eveleth, Minnesota. He even looked like a school teacher with his metal rim glasses and scholarly appearance. Without question, Henry's great love was the Canoe Base and the Quetico-Superior Country. He was an inspiration to all of the guides at the Base. His soft-spoken approach to the staff concealed an underlying iron-willed determination that earned the respect of everyone. He had a great knack for inspiring the younger guides by recounting feats of endurance that former guides had supposedly accomplished. A favorite yarn that he liked to recount was the evening paddle trip from the Base to the Paul Bunyan Tourist Shop on Hoist Bay in Basswood Lake and back again before midnight. The trip involved going west through Wind Lake to get to Basswood and Hoist Bay before dark, and then returning to the Base by paddling east on Basswood to Prairie Portage and then south to Moose Lake, a total distance of about 28 miles, hardly a leisurely evening jaunt. (Two other guys and I decided to try it anyway but we took a square-stern canoe and a 3 hp motor. We didn't get back to the Base until after midnight the next day.) Another favorite story was the day trip from the Base up to Canadian Agnes via the Shade and Silence Lakes and back via Sunday and Basswood. I never did try that one.

Henry echoed Cliff's remarks and urged me to stay at the Base and keep guiding. He suggested I take a crew on a more rugged trip like around Hunter Island as a kind of catharsis. To make it even more challenging he told me about a group of guides who had done the trip in just "four days." He also suggested that if time allowed, we might consider extending the Hunter Island route another 60 miles by turning north at Sturgeon and going to Beaverhouse and then back to Lac La Croix via the Quetico and Namakan Rivers rather than following the traditional route down the Maligne River. A lot would depend on the weather since going through Beaverhouse would add two days to the trip but it sure sounded interesting.

I also talked to Dave Ziegenhagan, the guide chief. He knew about the difficult trip I had just completed and he told me he would try to schedule me for another guiding trip as quickly as possible. It just happened that the guide who was scheduled to get a crew in two days was sick so I was assigned to take his place. Even though there were no restrictions on the size of the groups that entered the Quetico in 1958, the Canoe Base strongly recommended that the group size be limited to ten scouts and one adult leader. More people than that meant more food packs, tents and canoes and, from my point of view, more difficulty trying to make an arduous trip around Hunter Island in eight and one-half days.

My new crew arrived at the Base two days later about noon. I learned they were all from the Roswell, New Mexico area, and this was their first trip to the north country. They seemed to be a nice group of young men and it was an unexpected surprise to find only seven scouts and two adult leaders, both of whom were enlisted men in the Air Force. They were all explorer scouts and in good shape which meant we could probably take every portage in one or two trips which would save us valuable time on a long voyage. As we went through the usual preparations for our upcoming trip, I told the crew about the Hunter Island route and the challenge it presented. Without exception, they all wanted to give it a try, reserving the option to cut the trip short if we ran out of steam so to speak, or out of time. Later that afternoon, before the traditional beans and wiener supper, I talked to Henry and Dave to get their approval for our trip and asked if we could start our trip that evening after supper while we still had a couple of hours of light so as to get an earlier start the next day.

It took an approval from Cliff Hanson and a promise that I would never ask again, but we were allowed to begin our canoe trip just as the sun was beginning its final plunge into the western sky. Moose Lake was very calm as we paddled away from the Base, our canoes loaded for the long journey ahead. An hour and a half later, with the last lingering light of day, we set up our tents at the north end of New Found Lake on the big island campsite near the narrows going into Sucker Lake. Everyone was full of anticipation and excitement. I was thankful to the good Lord for giving me the opportunity to renew my faith in myself and I prayed it would be a good trip.

We were up before dawn the next morning, the first full day of our trip. Breakfast was light: cold milk and cereal, bread and jam, coffee and cocoa. Before heading east toward Knife Lake, which forms part of the southeastern edge of Hunter Island, we had to stop first at Prairie Portage, a good 30 minute paddle, to check

through Canadian Customs and get our Quetico travel permits and our fishing licenses at the Ranger Station.

Art Pattison, the Customs Agent, and his wife, Norma, were preparing breakfast when I knocked on the door of the Customs Cabin about 7 AM. I had met Art for the first time in 1957 when I stopped there on my Swamper trip and was happy to see him back for the 1958 season. We had visited a few weeks earlier when I had stopped by on my first two trips and were developing a nice friendship. Art was a career officer with Canadian Customs who normally worked as a Customs agent on the bridge over the Rainy River between Fort Frances and International Falls. (It was sometime in the late 1960's or early 1970's when the resident customs agents at the various Quetico entry points were replaced by a remote access computerized system which is in use today.)

Art had a distinctive British-Canadian accent, and with his wavy red hair and fair complexion, he seemed out of place among the rugged-looking characters who frequented his office during the summer. Always ready for a cup of tea and a "chat," his rather reserved appearance masked a wry sense of humor. Though he seemed out of place at Prairie Portage, I think he enjoyed the diversion it provided from working on the Bridge at Fort Frances. I apologized for stopping by so early but when I told Art about our planned trip he didn't seem too upset. Anyway I told him that I needed to get going so we signed the custom papers and I headed over to the Ranger Station for our fishing licenses and travel permit. I told Art that I would hopefully stop by in a couple of weeks and would have more time to talk.

The Canadian Ranger Station was about 100 yards east of the Customs Cabin and the occupants, Ranger Rod Salchert and his wife, Lee, nicknamed "Tiny," were about 180 degrees opposite in personality from Art and Norma. Rod seemed to me to be too young to be a Canadian Ranger (he was 19 at the time). I remember him as an enthusiastic and friendly free spirit who loved his work. He was also very popular with all the staff at the Canoe Base. "Tiny" was a diminutive gal who seemed to share Rod's enthusiasm although I think she found the isolation of Prairie Portage somewhat boring. She often helped Rod by filling out the fishing license applications. Her youthful beauty provided a nice excuse for the guides to stop by the Ranger Station for a visit. She and Rod made quite a team that summer of 1958. When I knocked on their door about 0730, they had just gotten up. They were kind enough to get our license applications filled out and give us our official Forest Travel Permit. I also delivered all the paperwork for the crews that would be coming by later that morning, and we were on our way.

An example of the Quetico Park Forest Travel Permit in August, 1961, signed by Ranger Rod Salchert. Photo by Jim Veenstra.

Our trip around Hunter Island really began when we left Prairie Portage. It was about 0830 by the time we paddled back east to the Birch Lake narrows. The sun had completely cleared the tops of the trees on the eastern shoreline. Our plan was to go as far as Cache Bay in Saganaga before sundown. That was probably

Visiting Knife Lake Dorothy on the Isle of Pines, July, 1958.

too much to expect for the first day and in fact, we didn't make it, partly because we stopped in Knife Lake to meet Dorothy Molter at her Isle of Pines Resort. But we did get as far as the eastern end of Ottertrack Lake, past the point where Benny Ambrose had his cabin. "Knife Lake Dorothy," as she was affectionately known, and Benny Ambrose, were the only people who had been allowed to remain living in the BWCAW after the 1964 Wilderness Bill was enacted. He and Dorothy were both named "Forest Service Volunteers" to resolve the controversy over their planned eviction. Benny died in 1982 and Dorothy died in 1986.

Everyone was tired and hungry by the time we set up camp on Ottertrack. We had actually made pretty good time paddling on Knife, going primarily in a northeasterly direction. The wind was not a factor. In the Quetico Park there are no designated campsites. I don't remember much about our first campsite except it was on the Canadian side of Ottertrack and that's where we "lost" our cooking utensils. We always followed a routine procedure for setting up camp. Each member of the crew was assigned a job. The quartermaster and his assistants put up the tents and unrolled and laid out the sleeping bags. The firemen gathered firewood and helped the cook gather rocks to build the fireplace. The cook got the pots and pans ready and hung the canvas rollup with the cooking utensils on a tree by the campfire. We also always said the "Wilderness Grace" before each meal: *"For food, for rainment, for life and opportunity, for sun and rain, for water and portage trails, for friendship and fellowship, we thank thee, Oh Lord, Amen."*

On day two we were up again at dawn. Our plan was to make it all the way to Kawnipi Lake. Everyone was tired and sore but after a breakfast of oatmeal, stewed fruit, canned Danish bacon, coffee and cocoa we felt revived. We made good time getting packed up and were soon on our way to Monument Portage, our first long portage of the trip. I'll never forget how unprepared I was for the soft mud and muck at the end of the portage. We had to wade knee-deep through the stuff to load the canoes. Fortunately, Cache Bay was very calm as we rounded the point and headed in a northwesterly direction toward the Silver Falls portage. Since the wind usually blows from the west in the Quetico, given the choice, it makes sense to start out long trips, if possible, with a tailwind. We had been blessed with favorable winds up to now. I just hoped that we would be toughened up by the time we encountered the inevitable headwinds that lay ahead.

I discovered that I had forgotten our cooking utensils at the Ottertrack campsite when we stopped at Boundary Point in Saganagons to make lunch. I looked in the kettle pack for a big mixing spoon to stir a concoction of Argentine corned beef and condensed milk for sandwiches. It sounds yucky and it tasted yucky. The spoon was nowhere to be found nor were any of our other utensils. We had been is such a rush to get packed up that morning that I failed to do a double check of the campsite before we left, a sign of my inexperience. All of our cooking utensils – mixing spoons, can opener, spatulas and silverware – were carefully tucked away in the canvas rollup which I could visualize tied securely to the pine tree at the Ottertrack campsite. I don't recall what I said but it wasn't "holy cow!" However, there was no thought of going back. We were committed to our itinerary so we decided to push on and make the best of the situation.

We made camp that night in Kawnipi near the entrance to McKenzie Bay. It was my first time going through the Falls Chain but we managed to get along unscathed. One of the crew members carved a wooden spoon from a piece of "beaver wood" (aspen) during the long paddle up Kawnipi from the last portage at Kennebas Falls. Since most of our hot meals were prepared in a big eleven quart kettle over an open fire, like the voyageurs used to do, the mixing spoon was an important tool though the voyageurs used a paddle to mix their stew. I had saved the corned beef can from our noon meal and managed to fashion a pretty good spatula by removing both ends and flattening the can and attaching a carved piece of wood as a handle with some wire I had brought along. The only real problem was the silverware and there we had to compromise. Some of the guys had brought along their own eating utensils and the rest of us either borrowed a fork or a spoon from someone or just used our fingers. We all adjusted pretty well once the initial shock of our loss had passed.

I was up before sunrise on Wednesday, our third day. I had not slept well in spite of my fatigue and sore muscles. The inability to sleep well on canoe trips has always been a problem for me. Sleeping on the hard ground was not comfortable even with the sleeping bag and the canvas ground cloth. None of us had air mattresses (they were considered too heavy to carry) and foam sleeping pads were not yet available. In spite of that, the scouts just accepted the privation of sleeping on the hard ground along with the mosquitoes and black flies, the long portages, wind and rain, and hours of paddling as the price for being in the wilderness. While there were only ten of us on this trip, five in each tent, the tents were hot and smelly inside and not really bug proof or even big enough. By the time we placed our sleeping bags side by side we were like sardines in a can. As a result, I often slept outside in the open or under my canoe or sometimes even on a table, as I did in this campsite, which had a large log table.

As the sun started creeping over the tree tops, I woke everyone and we got a fire going. The first two days of our trip had been very warm and even at this early hour the temperature was in the 70's. Everyone was pretty tired but a big breakfast put us all in a better frame of mind. We discussed the idea of temporarily giving up our quest and taking a layover day in Kawnipi to rest and reconnoiter and maybe forget about taking the side trip up to Beaverhouse but just do the Hunter Island circumference. If you look at the map, Sturgeon Lake is near the top of Hunter Island and is about the halfway point around the Island. If we took a layover day in Kawnipi and made it to Sturgeon by our fourth night, we would have reasonable chance to try for the Hunter Island loop. However we had to get to Sturgeon by our third day, today, if we hoped to make the side trip to Beaverhouse. Without question, I was guiding an unusual group of scouts. They all wanted to forge ahead, so we broke camp and headed north to Kawnipi Forks. We stopped for lunch on the Snake Falls portage at Keats Lake. By the time we paddled through the Russel Rapids and into the Sturgeon Narrows, it was late afternoon. We immediately encountered a strong headwind and it was a struggle to make any headway. We finally had to pull into shore to wait it out. My goal was to camp on the beautiful sandy beach campsite that juts out from the southern shore of Sturgeon about halfway down the lake. While we waited for the wind to calm, the crew cooked supper and we all rested. It was just after sundown before the wind subsided and we were able to shove off. Our way was illuminated by the afterglow in the western sky. The stars and moon were in full force by the time we set up our camp on the sandy beach campsite.

The following day, our fourth day, was beautiful, bright, and sunny. Because we had made such good time, I decided to take Henry Bradelich's advice and depart from the regular Hunter Island route down the Maligne River and instead head up to Beaverhouse. We indulged ourselves with a pancake and bacon breakfast and everyone took advantage of the beautiful sandy beach to swim and take a bath. The wind was blowing again but it was coming from the southeast and it literally blew us over to the Jean Creek portage on the north shore of Sturgeon to begin our journey to Beaverhouse. It was all new country to me and for the rest of the trip until we got back to Crooked Lake, I had to rely of my map and compass to find our way, rather than my memory. The fourth day was memorable for three reasons: the moose antler, the wind, and most important, paddling through the Milky Way.

We found the moose antler partially buried in the sand at the beginning of the Jean Creek portage. I was surprised that someone hadn't found it before us. The trip up the Creek into Burntside Lake was very pleasant. I recall seeing an old trappers cabin on an island in Burntside but we didn't stop to explore it. By the time we started paddling in Jean Lake the wind had shifted again, and was gusting from west to east and forming white caps on the lake. We had no trouble paddling to the point that separates the main part of Jean from the southern bay where the Burntside portage is located but we had a terrible time trying to go anywhere from there. Before going around the point to head west toward the Conk Lake portage, we all tightened our life jackets. It took us almost four hours of hard paddling along the north shoreline to go the three miles from that point to Conk Lake.

After a short paddle across Conk Lake, which was relatively calm, we portaged into Quetico Lake and were stopped from going any further. The wind was literally howling now and there were large white caps on the lake, much larger than we had encountered on Jean Lake. The Quetico Lake end of the portage was rocky, wide and dry, and since it was still early in the afternoon, probably no later than four or five o'clock, we decided to have an early supper and wait until the wind died down before moving on. We set up the reflector oven, rehydrated our apple slices and baked a two apple pies, rolling out the crust, comprised of flour, shortening and salt, on the bottom of one of the canoes. Our rolling pin was the cylindrical aluminum butter container. We then prepared a Spanish rice casserole and lemonade. It was was still pretty warm, probably in the mid eighties. By the time we were able to continue our journey, it was past sundown but still light enough to get oriented in a due westerly direction for the twelve-mile paddle to the western end of Quetico Lake, called *gwe taa maang* in Ojibway, meaning, "Sacred Land."

Sandy beach shoreline, Eden Island, Quetico Lake, where we camped on the fourth night of our trip. This view is looking west where the canoes are on the shore, July 1958.

We finally paddled out of the little bay where the portage was located and into the main body of the lake. The wind had vanished, and except for the occasional eerie sounds of the loons calling back and forth, a stillness had settled on the world. Our goal was to go as far down the lake as possible to maintain our schedule. I had no idea where we might find a campsite so we just started moving west. Our paddles dipped quietly into the clear water as the canoes glided silently along. The glassy surface of Quetico Lake suddenly became a reflecting mirror and I became aware that we were in different medium. We were surrounded by more stars than I had ever seen before or since, like we were paddling through the Milky Way. Then as if someone had turned on a huge light, the eastern sky started glowing with an iridescence that was almost blinding as the nearly full moon edged over the horizon behind us. We were all overwhelmed. It was one of those experiences that make you feel you're close to heaven if not actually there. It is almost indescribable, for words cannot portray the beauty or the significance of that moment. Inebriated by the celestial show we were watching, we paddled on for two or three hours and eventually found a campsite on the sandy beach of Eden Island.

We were awakened from our dreams on the morning of our fifth day by sunlight streaming into our tents. There were no rocks around to build a fireplace to cook breakfast so my crew from New Mexico, where they often camp in the desert, dug a hole in the sand for the fire and we we hung our pots for Farina and coffee on an improvised crossbar held up by two strong wooden stakes which were stuck in the sand. We got a late start but picked up a tailwind as

Cooking breakfast, Eden Island, Quetico Lake, day five, July 1958.

Portaging from Quetico Lake to Beaverhouse, day five, July 1958.

we headed across Beaverhouse Lake to the Quetico River. We noticed the Ranger cabin off to our left on the southern shoreline but we were moving so well we decided not to stop. We set up camp early that afternoon on a small island near the confluence of the Quetico and Namakan Rivers. We still had three and a half days to make it back to the Canoe Base. Everyone was feeling better since we were on the last stretch of our journey. Our food packs were lighter and our muscles were no longer aching as they had been.

We awoke to an overcast sky on the morning of our sixth day. It started raining while we were breaking camp and continued to rain intermittently as we paddled up the Namakan River toward Lac La Croix. For some reason, as we were going around the east side of Douglas Island in the Ivy Channel, my paddle suddenly snapped in half near the bottom of the loom. I had not hit it on any rocks, it just gave way. That had never happened before nor has it ever happened again in all my years of canoeing. That's one of the reasons we always carry an extra paddle in each canoe. It was still misting as we portaged around Snake Falls and passed by the Lac La Croix Ojibway Indian Village at the mouth of the river.

Lac La Croix was very calm and we passed by Twenty-Seven Island on the Minnesota side of the lake and set a course for Bottle Portage at the far southern end of the lake. The absence of wind was a nice change from the previous two days as big lakes can be extremely treacherous in the wind. The most direct route to the Bottle Portage and Iron Lake was to stay on the Minnesota side of Lac La Croix, and it was a good thing we did. It started raining harder as we were passing on the west side of Coleman Island. We were all soaked and getting chilled from the heavy rain that just would not stop. We were also hungry and I was concerned we were getting hypothermic. In those days there were a number of summer resorts on the Minnesota side of the lake. We decided to stop at one and try to dry out and maybe get some hot soup or coffee. Normally I would not have considered stopping but we were desperate. We managed to collect a total of five dollars from everyone and we probably owe our lives to the kind resort owner who allowed ten dirty, soaking wet and smelly young men into her kitchen. The five dollars was just enough for one bowl of soup for each person and five candy bars which we divided between the group. We must have waited there for an hour or so but it just kept raining so we finally left. After unloading our canoes and dumping all the water out, we started paddling again. We had to stop about every fifteen minutes and dump out the rainwater. It was unreal. We finally stopped for the day in a downpour on the Minnesota side of the lake across from the southern end of Irving Island. Everyone was so cold and tired that we just put up the two wet tents and the rain tarp and crawled into our soggy sleeping bags. After a while though, the rain finally stopped and the sun appeared in the western sky as it was near sunset. Everyone had warmed up a bit and we were ravenously hungry. We finally got a fire started and heated up some water for macaroni and cheese and hot chocolate. To this day, I still remember how thankful I was to have had that simple meal and how good it made me feel. I also realized for the first time an essential lesson to be learned from canoe trips or similar experiences. In this world of modern conveniences, over abundance and self-indulgence, one seldom has the opportunity to savor the basic needs that drive us all: a warm fire, a hot meal, a safe harbor and friends to share them with.

I don't think there was any rain left because the next day, our seventh day, the sun appeared right on schedule and by midmorning we had pretty much dried everything out. We took the Bottle Lake portage into Iron Lake and stopped to rest for awhile at Curtain Falls. We enjoyed a tailwind as we wound our way down Crooked Lake to Wednesday Bay where we camped at Table Rock. Monday, our eighth day, was relatively easy as we traveled up the Basswood River and over Horse Portage where we stopped for lunch. The sky was clear and there was a light westerly breeze as we paddled around US Point and on to Canadian Point where set up our last camp. We were up at dawn on the ninth and last day of our trip. After cleaning all the gear we paddled east to Prairie Portage and back to the Canoe Base via Sucker, New Found and Moose Lakes, arriving there in the late afternoon. We were just in time for a shower and sauna before the traditional turkey dinner and then the end of trip campfire at the Lodge with the other crews. After everyone recounted the trips they had taken, we all joined to say the closing prayer:

> "May the Great Master of All Good
> Scouts be With Us Until We Meet Again."

Each experience in life, both good and bad, adds to our character. Our trip around Hunter Island and to Beaverhouse was definitely a good experience but there were a few times when we were sorely tested and thought of giving up, but we didn't. In the years that have passed since that trip, I have forgotten the names of the crew who were with me and their face are only vague images in my memory. But that is not really important. They know who they are and what we accomplished. What is important is that we made the effort. We dared to challenge ourselves in spite of the very real possibility that we might not succeed. Even if we had failed to complete the trip at that time because of bad weather, injury or equipment malfunction it would not have mattered, for by the end of the second day we began to believe in ourselves and we knew we could do it. Henry Bradelich was right. The trip around Hunter Island was a catharsis. But it was also a revelation to me, an eighteen year old canoe guide, about the determination of the human spirit to overcome adversity and survive.

Sigurd F. Olson in his book, *The Lonely Land*, a story about his 500-mile canoe trip in 1955 through the wilds of Saskatchewen with five other men down the Churchill and Sturgeon-Weir Rivers, following the route of the French Voyageurs, summed up his *raison d'etre* as follows:

> If a man can pack a heavy load across a portage, if he can do
> whatever he has to do without complaint and with good humor,
> it makes little difference what his background has been. And
> if he can somehow keep alive a spark of adventure and romance
> as the old-time voyageurs seem to have done, then any expedition
> becomes more than a journey through wild country. It becomes a
> shining challenge and an adventure of the spirit. (1)

1. Sigurd F. Olson, The Lonely Land, Alford A Knopf, New York, 1964, p 16

* This story first appeared in the Fall 1988 issue of *the Boundary Waters Journal*.
It has been revised and expanded for this book

CHAPTER FOUR

Reflections On Canoeing In The Quetico
(A Few Quetico Highlights) *

I think almost anyone who has taken a canoe trip into the Quetico Provincial Park or the Boundary Waters Canoe Area would agree that it is a unique experience that beckons some of us to return again and again to answer the siren call of the wilderness. This place becomes part of our very being, a place where we can escape the stress of our modern life for a simpler existence, where you may not see another human being for days, where you can drink the water right out of the lake as I have done for sixty years (though now days it's safer to filter your drinking water), and where you can catch trophy fish from most of the lakes. There is nothing comparable to this area of more than two million acres of unspoiled glacial lakes and boreal forests on both sides of the international border, connected by age-old portages and streams through which you can travel, following many of the same routes that were used in the late sixteenth century when the first Ojibway Indians appeared[1], the French Voyaguers and explorers in the seventeenth and eighteenth centuries[2], and the modern-day travelers in the nineteenth and early twentieth centuries.[3]

I have often wondered about the meaning of the word, *Quetico*, and where it originated. It turns out it is an Ojibway word and there are a number of different meanings that have been associated with the word. The following definition seems to be generally acceptable. It comes from the Ojibway word, *gwe taa maang*. This refers to how the Ojibway view this area as "Sacred Land," and the place in the park named Quetico Lake, is occupied by "living spirits that have been there since time immemorial."[4] As I have traveled through the Quetico Park and the Boundary Waters Canoe Area over the years, I have often had a sense of entering a new world, like passing through a time warp, and I can sometimes feel the presence of those who have gone before.

As I have indicated elsewhere, I started guiding canoe trips in 1958 when I worked at Sommers Boy Scout Canoe Base on Moose Lake. During the three summers I worked there I guided a number of trips into the Quetico Park, roughly seven or eight each summer. The story of my trip around Hunter Island was

previously reported in Chapter Three. I would like to tell you about five other trips that I guided after the Hunter Island journey. But first let me tell you briefly about being a guide at Sommers Canoe Base during those years from 1958 to 1961.

When I started guiding I was eighteen years old, just out of high school, and caught up in the mystique of the history of the canoe country. I was full of vim and vigor and wanted to explore as many of the lakes in the Canoe Country as possible. Many of the Canoe Base guides at that time considered themselves modern-day French Voyageurs, like the rugged men who paddled their birchbark canoes and carried heavy bundles of furs over the portages in the seventeenth and eighteenth centuries. The primary goal of the Canoe Base trips then was to teach each crew of scouts how to function as a team and test their ability to meet the challenges of a wilderness canoe trip and become voyageurs. As guides, our job was to help them achieve that goal.

Trip 1: LOOKING FOR THE POWELL LAKE PORTAGE: JULY, 1961

Kawa Bay is a finger-like extension from the northeastern part of Kawnipi Lake. When you enter the Bay, it's just over three miles to the mouth of the Wawiag River where it enters Kawa Bay. The Ojibway name for the Wawiag River is *Kawawiagamok*. Kawa is thought to be the abbreviated form of Kawawiagamok.[5]

If you have ever been to Kawa Bay you'll recall there is something special about it. For one thing the water has a reddish-brown color, especially as you get near the mouth of the Wawiag. It also has an important historic significance to the Ojibway people due to the fact that many years ago there was an Ojibway Village located near the mouth of the Wawiag. Although it was fairly well established, according to Bill Magie as noted in the book about him by Dave Olesen, *A Wonderful Country*, the Village was forcibly abandoned in 1919 due to the influenza epidemic and the survivors were all moved to the Lac La Croix Indian Reservation by the Canadian Mounted Police and the Indian Service.[6] It is now off limits to camp there as we did in 1961 because the Provincial government has included the eastern end of Kawa Bay in the Wawiag River Nature Preserve (NR1).

I had heard a number of stories that were circulating around the Canoe Base about the Wawiag River and Mack Lake, which is accessible from the Wawiag. Powell Lake was mentioned but because if was out of the Quetico Park, and because one could fly into it, there wasn't much interest in going there via canoe. The only thing I knew about Kawa Bay at that time was the change in the color of the water near the mouth of the Wawiag and some vague story about the fact that at one time there had once been an Ojibway Indian Village there. So when I was assigned a crew of ten scouts in July, 1961, who were all members of their high school football team with their coach as the adult leader, I talked to them about going to Powell Lake. Their canoe trip was part of their training for the football season so they were anxious to take a difficult trip.

We had eight and one-half days to make the trip. We loaded our four canoes (two Seligas, one Grumman and one Old Town) with our Duluth Packs which included three food packs, one bread pack, four personal packs, one kettle pack with our cooking gear, my guide pack, three canvas tents, our life jackets, thirteen paddles, and our fishing gear.

On our first day we paddled from Moose Lake to Basswood and over the often muddy North Portage into Sunday lake and then across the two long but relatively easy Meadows Portages into Agnes Lake. We set up camp near Louisa Falls where the portage from Louisa Lake ends in Agnes. About halfway up the portage the falls have created a natural bath tub in the rocks. Unfortunately we didn't have time to bathe there. The next day we were up early and paddled up Agnes into Kawnipi via Bird, Anubis and McVicar Bay and into Kawa Bay where we camped on the island near the mouth of the Wawiag. We rested the next day, our third day. It was very hot, probably 90 degrees plus.

Camping with the scouts was different in 1958-1961 than the present day. It was somewhat reminiscent of canoe tripping in the early nineteen hundreds as related by Bill Magie.[7] Except for the rice, pasta and potato cubes, none of our food was dehydrated. We carried cans of bacon and vegetables and heavy sacks of flour, sugar, cornmeal, pancake mix, a three pound brick of American cheese and a 4 pound chunk of salami, plus numerous other items as noted in the picture of the "Wilderness Trail Food List." At each Quetico campsite we had to construct a large rock fireplace across which we laid a 2 to 3 inch diameter tree limb from which we would hang our cooking pots. A typical supper would

WILDERNESS TRAIL FOOD LIST

(Seven full days and two half days)

The following columns will provide the crew with a complete listing of all foods and corresponding food measurements that are to be drawn and packed during the outfitting at the Bay Post for Wilderness Canoe Trail use.

To use this listing effectively compare the food items with the weight and quantity list corresponding with the total number of members in the crew. If the crew has twelve persons, including the guide, pack slightly less than for totals of fourteen or sixteen. Use the same general procedure.

Read the following list very carefully before outfitting. Be certain that the food bags are properly marked and food packs ready to be utilized for packing.

Food Items	Quan. for 11 people	13 people	15 people
Apples	3 lbs.	3 lbs.	3½ lbs.
Apricots	1 "	1 "	1 "
Peaches	2 "	2 "	2¼ "
Prunes	3 "	4 "	5 "
Raisins	5 "	6 "	7 "
Oatmeal	4 lbs.	5 lbs.	6 lbs.
Farina	1½ "	2 "	2½ "
Corn Meal	2½ "	3 "	3½ "
Pancake Flour	6 lbs.	7 lbs.	8 lbs.
White Flour	9 "	10 "	10½ "
Potatoes	4 lbs.	4 lbs.	5 lbs.
Macaroni	2 "	2½ "	3 "
Spaghetti	2 "	2½ "	3 "
Rice	8 "	9 "	10 "
Barley	1 "	1 "	1 "
Corned Beef	3 cans (10 lbs.)	3 cans (10 lbs.)	3 cans (10 lbs.)
Spam	5 cans (4½ lbs.)	6 cans (5 lbs.)	7 cans (5½ lbs.)
Sausage	5 lbs.	5 lbs.	5 lbs.
Bacon	5 cans (4 lbs.)	5 cans (4 lbs.)	5 cans (4 lbs.)
Gravy Mix	¼ lbs.	¼ lbs.	¼ lbs.
Milk	2½ lbs.	2½ lbs.	2½ lbs.
Eggs	1¾ "	2 "	2¼ "
Cheese	5 lbs.	5 "	5 "
Butter	3 "	3 "	4 "
Canned Peas (303 can)	4 cans	4 cans	4 cans
Tomato Paste	8 cans	10 cans	12 cans
Onions (fresh)	6 lbs.	7 lbs.	8 lbs.
White Sugar	11 lbs.	12 lbs.	13 lbs.
Brown "	9 "	10 "	11 "
Cocoa	10 lbs.	12 lbs.	14 lbs.
Coffee	1 "	1 "	1 "
Tea	¼ "	¼ "	¼ "
Punch	2¾ "	3 "	3¼ "
Lemon Crystals	1 pkg. (12 oz.)	1 pkg. (12 oz.)	1 pkg. (12 oz.)
Cake Mix	7½ lbs.	7½ lbs.	7½ lbs.
Pudding Mix	4 "	4 "	4 "
Bread (fresh)	22 (loaves)	26 (1½ lb. loaves)	30 (loaves)
Holry	7 (boxes)	8 (boxes)	9 (boxes)
Jam	4 lbs.	4 lbs.	5 lbs.
Peanut Butter	4 lbs.	4 lbs.	5 lbs.
Shortening or Lard	3 lbs.	3 lbs.	3 lbs.
Salt	1½ "	1½ "	1½ "
Saccharin	80 (tablets)	80 (tablets)	80 (tablets)
Cinnamon	4 oz.	4 oz.	4 oz.
Pepper	2 oz.	2 oz.	2 oz.
Baking Powder	8 oz.	8 oz.	8 oz.
Mapleine	4 oz. (liquid)	4 oz. (liquid)	4 oz. (liquid)

(Extra non-listed items, if desired - - - - - - - - - - - - - - - - -

Extra, essential items:

Matches (in water tight can)	100 (stick matches)	100 (stick matches)	100 (stick matches)
Bar Soap (small bar)	5 (bars)	5 (bars)	5 (bars)
Bon Ami (small bar)	1 (bar)	1 (bar)	1 (bar)
Chore Girls (wire mesh)	6	6	6
Toilet Paper	2 (rolls)	2 (rolls)	2 (rolls)
THE TOTAL WEIGHT OF FOOD	225 lbs.	233 lbs.	240 lbs.

Each person on the canoe trails consumes about 2¼ lbs. of food per day or 18 lbs. per week. Two pounds is very adequate for daily trail food consumption; however, Explorer Scout age Young MEN usually require a little more food than the average person.

Sommers Canoe Base Trail Food List, 1961. Photo by Jim Veenstra.

be some type of stew or pasta, corn bread or cake baked in our reflector oven, pudding, coffee and lemonade or Kool Aid. Breakfast would be real oatmeal or farina or pancakes and bacon, stewed fruit, coffee and cocoa. Lunch usually consisted of sandwiches of salami and cheese or peanut butter and jam or canned corned beef mixed with evaporated milk, all spread on one of the 25 loaves of compressed Master Bakery white bread, plus Kool Aid. One of the goals of the Region Ten Canoe Base trips was to teach the scouts wilderness cooking skills. The Wilderness Cookery book was given to each crew to help in planning the meals.[8]

When we set up camp, each crew member had an assigned job, again part of the plan to help teach the scouts to work together as a team. The cook and his

SUGGESTED NINE DAY TRAIL MENU

(Seven full days, two-half days on trails)

The purpose of the following suggested menu is to assist the crew in working out the adequate day-by-day menu plan. This menu is by no means required, only inserted to relate to the crews the possibilities of crew menu planning and actual cooking participation.

FIRST DAY

Breakfast	Lunch (First meal on trails)	Supper
(at the base)	Bread and butter Peanut butter and jelly	Boundary Stew Rice pudding (Swedish)
	Cheese and sausage Grape punch Candy	Cocoa Corn bread (save ½ of C. bread for lunch)

SECOND DAY

Breakfast	Lunch	Supper
Fruit stew Oatmeal Cocoa	Bread and butter Cheese and sausage Corn bread and jam Lemonade Raisins	Potatoes and gravy Fried spam White cake or spice Apple sauce Holry and jam

THIRD DAY

Breakfast	Lunch	Supper
Prunes Farina Bacon Cocoa	Bread and butter Peanut butter and jam Cheese White cake or spice Lemonade	Spanish rice Apple pie or Chocolate pudding Cocoa and coffee Holry and brown sugar

FOURTH DAY

Breakfast	Lunch	Supper
Fruit stew Oatmeal Cocoa	Bread and butter Sausage Jam Holry and brown sugar Apricots Grape Punch	Macaroni & cheese Spice cake Peaches Cocoa and tea

FIFTH DAY

Breakfast	Lunch	Supper
Apple sauce French toast Syrup Bacon Cocoa	Cheese on hot toast Spice cake with raisins Orange punch	Kala Mojka Rice pudding Apple cake Coffee and tea Holry and brown sugar

SIXTH DAY

Breakfast	Lunch	Supper
Peaches Farina Baking powder biscuits Bacon Cocoa	Fish sandwiches (if any left) Sausage & cheese Baking powder biscuits Jam and butter Lemonade	Pack Sack stew Apple sauce Ginger bread cake Butterscotch pudding Cocoa and tea Holry & brown sugar

SEVENTH DAY

Breakfast	Lunch	Supper
Prunes Oatmeal Corn bread Bacon Cocoa	Bread and butter Jam and peanut butter Sausage Lemonade or punch Raisins	Spaghetti Italienne Spotted dog Bannock Chocolate cake Tea and coffee

EIGHTH DAY

Breakfast	Lunch	Supper
Fruit stew Pancakes and syrup Bacon Cocoa	Bread and jam Sausage and cheese Grape punch Apricots Chocolate cake	Potatoes Au Gratin Fried beef & gravy Rice pudding Flop Jocks Cocoa and tea Holry and brown sugar

NINTH DAY

Breakfast	Lunch	Supper
Peaches Oatmeal Cocoa Bread pudding	Bread and jam Peanut butter Grape punch	at the base

Sommers Canoe Base Nine Day trail meal menu, 1961. Photo by Jim Veenstra.

assistant prepared the meals once the fireplace was erected. The quartermaster and his assistants set up the tents and the ground covers which were the tent floors. The Base supplied the sleeping bags which were cleaned after each trip. The bags were laid directly on the canvas ground covers as we did not have air mats. Firemen gathered firewood (the best being dry aspen – "beaver wood" – or dry cedar) and the latrine detail dug a potty hole back in the woods and helped with the firewood. The canoes were placed upside down away from the shoreline each night. The cook often used an upturned canoe for a table to prepare meals. The dishwashing detail cleaned all the pots and pans in hot soapy water away from the lake and rinsed everything with hot water and put the pots on top of an

upturned canoe under which we stored the food packs. If a bear tried to get to the food packs it would have to move the canoe which would cause the pots and pans to fall off and make a noise. In all my years of guiding I never hung a food pack in a tree, and I only had one bear attack the food packs.(The first and only time was in 1964. See Chapter Six, Trip One.)

Day three, our layover day, was bright and sunny and very hot. By noon the temperature was in the high eighties or low nineties. I took a few of the guys over to look at the site of the old Ojibway Village. Some of the guys went fishing but it was so hot we all headed back to camp for an early lunch. As soon as we opened the bread pack to make sandwiches we noticed a terrible odor. When we had packed the bread pack back at the Base there was a choice of taking all white bread as we usually did, or whole wheat bread. I opted for fifteen loaves of wheat bread plus ten loaves of white bread. That turned out to be a big mistake. The odor we smelled was molding wheat bread. It was all ruined plus a couple of the loaves of white bread. We had to bury the stuff to get rid of the odor. That left us with about six loaves of bread plus seven boxes of Holry crackers for the rest of the trip plus whatever corn bread we could bake if we had time.

We started up the Wawiag on the fourth day of our trip, planning to camp in Powell Lake that night. The thing we noticed at first as we entered the river was the change in the types of trees lining the banks of the river. There was an abundance of oak and maple trees which formed a canopy of branches and leaves in places over the generally quiet-flowing river. I also remember two shallow rapids where we had to walk our canoes through. We paddled for a few hours, following the serpentine twists of the river until we came to the Mack Creek, which

Walking canoes through shallow rapids, Wawiag River.

flowed into the Wawiag from Mack Lake, about five miles from Kawa Bay. We still had a long way to go before we found, what I hoped was the portage into Powell Lake. I was somewhat anxious about finding the portage since there was none marked on any of our maps. But I felt sure that a big lake like Powell had to have a portage into the Wawiag. By late afternoon we still had not found the portage. We had passed the place where the Greenwood River entered the Wawiag and the place further up stream where the river divided but still no portage. Reluctantly we decided to set up camp on the river bank where it was only about ten feet wide. I felt we were close to Powell Lake but if there was portage, it wasn't used very often. I told the guys that if we couldn't find the portage the next day we would have to go back to the Mack Creek and return to the Canoe Base via Mack Lake.

Walking along shoreline, Powell Lake, looking for the portage to the Wawiag River.

The next morning we were up early. After a quick breakfast, I took my Old Town canoe and three of the scouts and our gear and went back down the river to a place we had noticed the day before where there was a small bay on the south side of the river. Meanwhile the rest of the crew packed up the camp and they were to follow us downstream and look for where my canoe was secured and wait for us there. Using a compass, we started walking through the woods in a southerly direction toward where we thought Powell Lake should be. I have to admit we were very lucky. As we reached the crest of a hill we could see Powell Lake off to the south. We walked toward the lake and finally got to the north shoreline. I decided that if we walked along the north shore we would hopefully find the portage, which I felt had to be there. It took about an hour but we finally found it. It wasn't very well used but it was surprisingly clear and definitely was not a game trail. We followed it uphill and finally ended close to where the rest of the crew was waiting by my canoe. We had missed it the first time because the Wawiag end of the portage was overgrown with shrubs and blueberry bushes.

By the time we portaged into Powell the sunlight was fading. Because of the time lost looking for the portage, we decided to push on after checking out the island campsite. We left Powell going east on the Greenwood River which involved a couple of portages. It was dark when we started the last portage into Windblown Lake and we had to use our flashlights to follow the trail which was well-used and open. We made camp at the end of the portage about midnight. After a supper of sandwiches and cookies, we set up the tents and sleeping bags and went to bed.

We got a late start the next day, out sixth, and just managed to pack up the camp before the rain started. We paddled in a constant drizzle from Windblown to Term Lake and then over a series of seven portages on the Ross Creek and into Ross Lake where we found a campsite, again in the dark. We were all thoroughly soaked and tired but no one complained. The euphoria of what we had accomplished thus far was like a tonic.

The next day, the sun was shining. We paddled down Saganagons to Lilypad Lake and then into Juniper and finally camped on Ottertrack Lake at dusk. On our eighth day we paddled down Knife Lake to the Isle of Pines and visited with Dorothy Molter, known affectionately as the Root Beer Lady or Knife Lake Dorothy. It was a real treat to visit with her. Everyone enjoyed a bottle of her homemade ice-cold root beer before moving on to camp in Carp Lake. We finally made it back to the Canoe Base in the early afternoon of our ninth day. It had been a difficult trip, anxiety inducing at time but also satisfying, knowing we had come together to accomplish our goal, even maybe taking on the persona of the French Voyageurs.

Trip 2: POOHBAH LAKE, August, 1959

Poohbah is a big lake, 2370 acres, according the information supplied by the Quetico Park Headquarters in Atikokan.[9] It is situated on the northeastern edge of Hunter Island. When I started working at the Canoe Base I heard various stories about what a beautiful lake it was as well as great fishing lake. It was a popular

place for parties to fly into for a day of fishing in the nineteen forties and fifties. This practice slowed down quite a bit with the airplane restrictions put in by the Provincial Government in 1954, somewhat in concert with the airplane ban in the BWCA signed by President Truman in 1949.[10,11] The First Nation Indians at Lac La Croix were an exception to the no-fly rule and are still allowed to guide seaplane parties into Poohbah for a day of fishing.[12] That practice came to a halt about 2018 when Campbell's Resort on Lac La Croix, who supplied the planes, got out of the seaplane business and sold all of their airplanes.[13] Even though I was aware of the possibility in 1959 that an airplane full of fishermen flying in for a day might show up, the lake intrigued me and I really wanted to go there. The Ojibway name for the lake is *Gan dook gwe mawitay*, which means, "place for getting bark for canoes."[14] The English name, Poohbah Lake, goes back to 1896. It is the name of one of the characters in the Gilbert and Sullivan play, *The Mikado*.[15]

I noticed that very few if any of the guides from the Canoe Base took crews into Poohbah, partly because it's difficult to get into unless you fly in or come in from one of the resorts on Lac La Croix via motor boat to the Maligne River and paddle up to Tanner Lake and go up the Poohbah Creek as I did in 1974 and 1995. Most of the time if a crew made it to Tanner Lake going east they would either continue down the Maligne River to Lac La Croix or take the Tanner Portage into the Darky Creek and then into Darky Lake, now called Darkwater Lake. I decided that I wanted to take a trip into Poohbah and the opportunity presented itself in 1959, my second year of guiding at the Base. I was assigned to a crew of 9 explorer scouts and their adult advisor from Colorado who wanted to take a challenging canoe trip. I suggested we go to Poohbah and they agreed.

There are four portages into Poohbah marked on the Canadian Ranger Map, one from the east, one from the south and two from the west. The easiest canoe trip access to Poohbah is from Lac La Croix on the east, up the Maligne River for a short distance into Tanner Lake and then into Poohbah via the Poohbah Creek. There is also a portage from Wink Lake that is east of Poohbah but it is a difficult, long and an unmarked forty-five degree downhill slope from Wink through underbrush and fallen trees.

Going up to Wink from Poohbah is even worse, as I discovered years later. I chose to go into Poohbah by coming from the east via Allen and Bernice Lakes. The portage from the south is from Conmee and is a series of three portages which total about two and half miles in length.

We departed from the Canoe Base on the morning of August sixth: nine scouts, one adult advisor and me. Our canoes were loaded with three food packs, one bread pack, one kettle pack, three tents, life jackets, paddles, fishing gear, three personal packs, my personal pack and a flotilla of three Seliga wood/fiberglass canoes and one Old Town wood/canvas canoe. We stopped briefly at Prairie Portage to check through customs and pick up our Quetico Travel Permit and fishing licenses. We spent our first night camped at the north end of North Bay. The next day we had pretty easy going into Kahshahpiwi via Isabella and Side Lakes and stopped there for lunch. We then pushed on through Keffer and Sark and made camp for the night in Carin Lake. Our plan was to make it to Fred Lake on our third day and into Poohbah on the fourth day, giving us time to spend a couple of layover days in Poohbah before heading back to the Canoe Base.

We got an early start on day three. The weather was very favorable as we portaged into Heronshaw then into Metacryst and Baird Lakes. We took the long portage from Baird into Keats and took a break at Split Rock Falls where we stopped for lunch before going into Chatterton. It started to cloud over and the wind started blowing from the west as we portaged into Russel Lake from Chatterton. We had to paddle against a steady head wind as we crossed Russel to the portage into Sturgeon and it started raining by the time we finished the portage. Everyone was getting tired so we found a campsite in Heron Bay and called it a day. Up to this point in the trip we had not seen any other people since we had left North Bay, and as it turned out, we didn't see anyone until the very end of our trip. Even though we were all experiencing the rigors of the trip, the level of enthusiasm was still positive. It was a good thing because the following day was probably the most difficult day of the whole trip.

I had been through all the lakes we had traversed thus far but now we were in unknown territory for me. The Canadian Ranger map suggested that Allen Creek, from Fred Lake into Allen Lake, was navigable and that's where we began our fourth day. The weather had cleared and the sun was shining as we portaged into a small pothole and then into the Creek itself. From the map it looked like the distance from Fred to Allen was about three miles but when we finally got to Allen it seemed to be a lot longer. We encountered difficulties almost as soon as we started in the creek. In addition to four brush-filled poorly used portages, the creek was full of fallen trees and beaver dams which blocked our path. The water level was fine in most places but in order to progress we had to move the trees or saw them in half, and slide the canoes over the beaver dams.

It took most of the day to get into Allen Lake. The sun was still bright and about 40 degrees above the horizon as we paddled across Allen to the portage into Bernice. I don't recall seeing any campsites in Allen but we really weren't looking for one. Our goal was to get to Poohbah before dark and camp there. The sun was fading by the time we finished the portage into Bernice. Even though we had stopped briefly in Allen for lunch, every one was tired and getting hungry. I suggested that we stop and camp in Bernice and go into Poohbah the next day but the crew wanted to keep going. We took the half-mile portage into Poohbah in semi-darkness. When we finished the portage it was very dark. There was no moonlight, only the stars to light our way. I had no idea where a campsite might be located. The map showed a couple of islands about a mile due west from the portage so we started paddling in that direction. As we headed out into the black void, I realized it was a dumb decision on my part not to have stayed in Bernice.

When we reached the islands, we paddled around the south end of the larger one, using our flashlights to illuminate the shoreline. We finally found an area that looked like a campsite and on closer inspection that proved to be the case. It was after midnight by the time we got a fire going and a pot of stew cooking and the tents erected. It had been a long day and everyone was exhausted. With the morning light we could see that the campsite we had chosen was not where we wanted to spend the next two days so after breakfast we packed everything and looked for a better place, which turned out to be on the smaller island just to the north. By noon we had our new camp set up, and after a quick swim to get some of the grime off, we went fishing. We headed southwest toward where the Wink Lake portage was marked on the map. Using red and yellow jigs and spoons we immediately started catching medium sized walleyes. As soon as we unhooked a fish and dropped the line back in the water another walleye took the bait. It was unreal and unexpected. We released all the fish except the ones we saved for a walleye dinner that night and the next.

Everyone had a great time in Poohbah so it was with reluctance that we packed up and left for home on day seven, going by way of the three long portages from the south end of Poohbah into Conmee Lake. All together they amounted to about two and half miles of hiking. Other than being long and laborious, the crew moved along very well and we were in Conmee by early afternoon. When we got to Brent we picked up a tailwind so we lashed our canoes together, and using our tarp for a sail, had a fast ride to the McIntyre portage. We continued to enjoy the tailwind across most of McIntyre to the Sarah Lake portage. We camped that night in Sarah on a sandy beach campsite and made it to North Bay the following day, our eighth day, and stayed in one of my favorite campsites, situated in a cedar grove on the south end of North Bay opposite United States Point.

On the last day of our trip we headed south to Wind Bay and portaged into Wind Lake, then across Wind to the portage into Moose Lake and due east across Moose to the Canoe Base. After we cleaned out the canoes and put all our gear back in the F.A Bean Bay Post, everyone took a shower and sauna. A turkey dinner and a campfire in the Lodge finished off the night. I said goodbye to the guys the next morning as they loaded up their bus for the trip back to Colorado. I was sad to see them leave as it had been a great trip.

My interest in Poohbah brought me back there again in 1974 and in 1995. On both occasions I came in from the west via Lac La Croix. The 1974 trip was with my two young sons and two friends and their sons from Duluth. On that trip we took a bus portage from Crane Lake to Lac La Croix and then our three aluminum canoes were pulled in tandem by motor boat from Zup's Resort on Lac La Croix to the Maligne River. The 1995 trip was with my cousin, Chuck Mertensotto and two friends from Illinois, Bill Lorenzen and Tom Wilson. We flew from Crane Lake to Campbells Resort on Lac La Croix where we were met by Jay

Standing on the dock at Campbell's Resort getting ready for motor boat tow to Maligne River on the way to Poohbah. From left to right: John Dailey, Bill Lorenzen, Jay Handberg, owner of Campbell's Resort, Chuck Mertensotto and Tom Wilson, September 1995. Photographer unknown.

Handberg, the resort owner. His staff towed our canoes to the Maligne River. We camped in Poohbah on both trips in the campsite I had stayed in with the scouts in 1959. We had fantastic fishing as before but in addition to walleyes, we caught big northerns and lake trout. The trip in 1995 was when we found the portage from Poohbah to Wink which I couldn't locate in 1959 or in 1974. My friend, Tom Wilson, found it. It was almost impassable. We also found a beautiful sandy beach swimming site near our campsite.

Trip 3: DELAHEY LAKE: FIRST VISIT 1958

When I started guiding in 1958, I spent a lot of time looking at maps of the Quetico and the BWCA to determine which lakes might be off the beaten track a bit and make for interesting destinations for future canoe trips. As I said in an earlier chapter, I would like to be have been able to visit all the lakes but that would just not be possible so I had to make choices. One of the lakes that I really wanted to see was Delahey. Situated due west from Conmee, one of my favorite lakes, it was definitely off the beaten track and while not inaccessible, would require a lot of work to get to it. It was named after George Delahey, a life-long member of the Department of Lands and Forests and former Quetico Park supervisor.[16]

The Base had a special building for the guides to gather between trips, "the Teepee." I used to hang around there and talk with the older guides about some of the lakes I wanted to visit, including Delahey. None of them had been there but they mentioned the story about F. B. Hubachek Sr., who founded the Quetico-Superior Wilderness Research Center on Basswood Lake and who reportedly, some years before, had cut the portages from Delahey to Conmee that were marked on the map. Well, that was enough to really pique my interest and resolve to go to Delahey. I was able to do this at the end of August, 1958, with my last crew for the season.

The crew of Scouts were all from Cincinnati, Ohio. There were 9 scouts and 2 adult advisors. We started our trip from the Base around August 12th. The itinerary for our trip was to go to Conmee and set up a base camp and spend a day with three scouts to go over the long portage to Delahey with one canoe and spend a few of hours there exploring the lake before returning to Conmee the same day. Not knowing what to expect regarding the portage, I didn't think taking the whole crew there would be a good idea. Instead of taking all wooden canoes on this trip we took two Grumman aluminum canoes which weighed less and would make for easier carrying over the long portage into Delahey.

We camped our first night in North Bay. There is a small unnamed lake between Kahshahpiwi and Joyce Lake where we hoped to camp on day two. Following the usual route through Isabella and Side Lakes to the long portage into Kahshahpiwi, we made good time, arriving in Kahshahpiwi before noon. I had carried my canoe and personal pack over the portage and went back for another load. I was about half way through the portage for the second time when I noticed something lying in the brush a few yards to the left of the portage. I took off my pack and walked

Dead fawn found on the portage into Kahshahpiwi coming from Side Lake, August 1958.

over to the object and found a fawn that had been shot in the chest. The carcass was still warm and the blood had not yet congealed. Just about that time one of the adult advisors came along carrying a pack and I called him over. We were both dumbfounded and angry. Who would shoot a fawn and where were they? We had not seen anyone else on the portage either coming from Kahshahpiwi or going to it nor had we heard any gunshots. After some debate we decided to skin the fawn and take the hind quarters and cook them that night. We cut off as much of the meat as we could and wrapped it in some aluminum foil that we had. I folded up the hide and put it in one of the packs, thinking I would clean it and do something with it, which I did when I got back home after the season. After lunch we paddled the four miles to the portage into the unnamed lake and set up camp. I can't remember what kind of stew we cooked up that night but I do remember roasting some of the venison over the fire and wrapping pieces of seasoned venison in our aluminum foil and cooking it in coals left over from our fire. Thinking about it now and how good it tasted still makes my mouth water. We decided that the person who shot the fawn must have gone over the portage at least an hour or so before we got there and continued on up Kahshahpiwi after the incident.

On day three we took the portage into Joyce Lake from the pot hole and then into Marj, Burt and the Darkwater River into Suzanette and finally into Conmee. We headed for the very northeastern part of the lake, very close to where the portage started into Delahey. There were no campsites there so we built one near the northern tip of Conmee, high above the shoreline. In fact we had to construct a log ladder from the shoreline up to our campsite. Our plan was to take three layover days to rest and fish and on one of the days take a day trip into Delahey.

I hung up the fawn hide and tried to scrape it clean and let it dry. Never having dealt with an animal hide before I wasn't sure what to do. I eventually made a vest from it as noted in the accompanying picture. I still have the vest though I am

The ladder we built at our campsite in Conmee. Photo by Bill Smith.

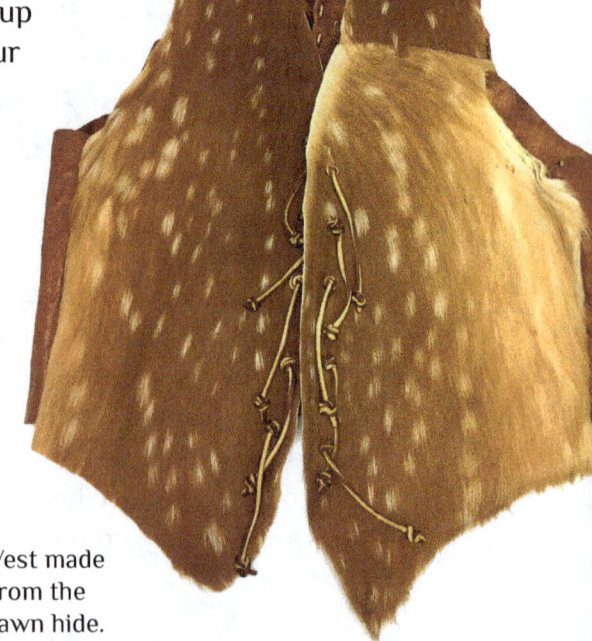

Vest made from the fawn hide.

Three scouts who made the trip over the long portage to Delahey Lake which is in the background.

sad to say I have outgrown it.

We spent out first layover day resting and fishing and planning our day-trip to Delahey. We left early the next morning, our fifth day with our lunch, one aluminum canoe and three scouts. We planned to spend the day in Delahey and get back to Conmee before dark. I don't remember much about the portages except they was mostly flat and dry and had not been used much. At times it was hard to follow but there were old blazes on the trees that helped and we added a few blazes of our own. We finally made it to Delahey around noon and paddled due east about half a mile to an island where there was a beautiful campsite with a table. On the table there was a sealed jar with a few messages from previous campers. One in particular was from F.B. Hubachek Jr. and was dated July, 1951.

Table on Delahey Lake campsite built by H.B. Hubachek Jr. In 1951, as it appeared in 1958. A glass jar with messages from previous visitors is on the table.

He gave his address and told about how he and some friends had built the table in 1951 and had cut the portage from Delahey to Conmee, the one we had just traversed, in 1950. I don't remember the other messages but I did write his name and address down and wrote to him in early September, 1958, when I got back home to Illinois, The story that I had heard before that the portages were made by F.B. Hubachek Sr. was obviously incorrect.

I was surprised and happy to receive a very kind and informative letter from Mr. F.B. "Bill" Hubachek, Jr. dated September 10, 1958 which I still have and which I'm referring to in writing this account.[17] He was the son on F.B. Hubachek, Sr. and was a lawyer in his father's law firm, Hubachek and Kelly, in Chicago. It was his father, as I mentioned earlier, who had established the Quetico-Superior Wilderness Research Center on Basswood Lake in 1948 and which is now part of the University of Minnesota.[18] Bill told about how he first started "...tripping into the Quetico starting in 1931..." and how he was attracted to Delahey because "...it looked like nice country and was remote and wild..." In order to get to Delahey, he and a group of friends "...came in from the north (from Camel lake) in 1950... following the route of the Creek which flows from Veron Lake through what we have named Gilbert Lake and down into Camel." He said the "...Creek is very difficult traveling because it involves several carries and you frequently find yourself on swampy mud flats over which it is almost impossible to navigate by canoe. It was a tremendous effort..." From Veron Lake they, "... cut a six-chain portage to the pothole just north of Delahey." He commented that, "Delahey Lake and the island campsite thereon are among my favorites." They left Delahey in 1950 by cutting the long portages to Conmee Lake that are now listed on the Canadian Ranger Map as the "Death March Portages." He said they returned to Delahey in 1951 and constructed the table on the campsite where we had eaten our lunch, and did more work clearing the portages they had established. He mentioned one other interesting thing in his letter. They discovered a blaze on a jack pine along the shore of Delahey in 1950 and found a tin can at the base of the tree which had a note from Roger Miller, one of the older guides at Sommers Canoe Base. Bill said Miller reported that "...he had explored the area between Conmee and Delahey on foot in 1950, and had not brought the canoes..." Mr. Hubachek said, "That winter I corresponded with Roger Miler, and the next year he took a party to Delahey over my trails." Bill sent me a brief followup letter dated September 17, 1958, in which he mentioned there was a "nice tent site right in the middle of the Delahey Lake Island...and a trail from the table running back to the tent site."[19] He also included a hand-written map of the portages he had made but I lost it somewhere along the way.

We spent our third layover day, the sixth day of our trip, fishing and exploring Conmee, and headed back to the Base on day seven, through Brent and McIntyre to Cecil Lake where we camped for the night. On day eight we headed south through Tuck and Kett Lakes into Ranger Bay of Basswood and camped across from United States Point in North Bay in the middle of a cedar grove. On day nine we cleaned up all the gear and made it back to the Base in mid afternoon via Wind Lake, my favorite route to Moose Lake from Basswood.

Trip 4: DELAHEY LAKE: SECOND VISIT - 1961

I didn't make it back to Delahey again until 1961, my last year of guiding for the Base. This time I followed the route taken initially by Bill Hubachek as described above, coming from the north, from Fred Lake. We left the Base and headed

north through Kahshahpiwi, Keffer, and Sark and then through Cutty, Metacryst and Baird to Keats Lake, and then into Chatterton and Russel and then into Heron Bay and finally into Fred Lake. We camped on a beautiful sandy beach in Fred where there were some iron stoves and other stuff left behind from the logging days.

We then followed what is now called the Cutty Creek into Nag Lake and finally into Camel Lake. My plan was to follow the portages that Bill Hubachek had cut from Camel into Delahey and camp in Delahey on the island campsite with the table that he had built in 1951. Looking back I don't recall the portage from Camel into the lake he named, "Gilbert" as being too difficult, just long. We stayed one night in Delahey and then took the long portages into Conmee where we camped for the night and had time for some walleye fishing that evening. We made it back to the Base in plenty of time for the traditional turkey dinner on day nine.

Delahey is definitely and out-of-the-way lake but I'm not sure it's worth the effort to get there other than to say you've been there. From a fisherman's perspective, Bill Hubachek commented in his letter of that he caught some northern pike but he fished extensively for Lake Trout and had no success. In any case, I'm glad I went there and had a chance to touch base with a real gentleman, Mr. F.B. "Bill" Hubachek, Jr.

TRIP 5: Meadows Lake and the "Lost" Canoe

My third guiding trip in the summer of 1959 for Sommers Canoe Base began in early July. The group consisted of ten explorer scouts, one adult advisor and me. We planned to camp our first night in lower Agnes and then move on to Kawnipi for a couple of days and then return to the Canoe Base via the Falls Chain, Saganagons and Knife Lake. The weather was ideal and we made good time to Sunday Lake where we stopped for lunch. As we paddled out into the lake we could see a flotilla of canoes down the lake heading for the first Meadows Portage, their apparent destination, Agnes Lake, the same as ours. There must have been sixteen or seventeen aluminum canoes, a few of which were 15 footers. Most of the group were college-age men and women and the canoes were all from Bill Rom's Canoe Country Outfitters (CCO).

By the time we got to the Meadows portage most of their group had already

started over the portage. To avoid a lot of confusion I decided to have some of our guys help move things along by carrying some of the other group's packs over the portage, leaving the rest of our crew to start carrying our stuff. By the time we got our four canoes and packs to the end of the portage, the other group had gone on to the second portage from Meadows into Agnes Lake. The only unusual thing was one of their 15 foot canoes was still sitting at the end of the portage along with the paddles. I figured they would be coming back for it so we just left it there and decided to camp in Meadows rather than going on to Agnes. With all those people ahead of us it might have been difficult to find a campsite.

We were up early the next morning as we wanted to get to Kawnipi early to find a campsite and have some time for fishing. As we paddled past the portage from Sunday Lake on our way to the portage into Agnes, I noticed that the canoe from the day before was still sitting there. I was unsure what to do and upset that the folks who left it there hadn't come back for it. How could you leave a canoe behind? I decided I didn't want someone to steal Rom's canoe so I pulled into the shore and had a couple of the scouts help me carry the canoe into the woods to hide it. I figured when I got back to Ely after our canoe trip I would go to CCO and tell Bill what I did and where to find the canoe.

It was around 0900 when we got into Agnes and started the long paddle up to the Agnes River East Channel through Bird, Anubis and McVicar Bay into Kawnipi. There was no sign of the large group as we headed north. They seemed to have disappeared. Maybe they portaged into Louisa or maybe into East Lake. One thing was sure: they didn't come back for their canoe, and I never did find out what eventually happened to them except as you'll see below, they did report the lost canoe to CCO.

About ten days after I hid the canoe in the woods, I was able to go into Ely and immediately went to CCO to tell Bill about the canoe and where to find it. Both Bill and his wife, Barbara, were there. As soon as I started telling them about the canoe, Barbara started yelling at me. She was mad and let me know that what I had done was a bad thing. She said it took two of her guys a whole day to find the canoe. I felt really bad and apologized to her but she was angry. Then Bill spoke up and told her to quiet down, that I was only trying to protect their property and he thanked me and gave me a Hudson Bay ax and sheath as a reward. God bless her, Barb had a right to be mad, and I felt really stupid for hiding the canoe. I apologized again and we parted friends. In fact Bill hired me to guide canoe trips for him during the summer of 1962. If there is a moral to this story it might be, "Mind Your Own Business."

REFERENCES:

(1). Historic Fort Snelling, Native American Exhibit, Minnesota Historical Society

(2). Grace Lee Nute, The Voyageur, Minnesota Historical Society, St. Paul, 1955. pp. 3-10

(3). Shirley Peruniak, Quetico Provincial Park, An Illustrated History, Friends of Quetico Park, 2000.

(4). Explanation given by the Lac La Croix First Nation leadership as noted in the Quetico Preliminary Management Plan of 2017.

(5). Lake Names of Quetico Provincial Park, Monograph of Friends of Quetico Park, 2013. p.5

(6). Dave Olesen, A Wonderful Country. The Quetico-Superior Stories of Bill Magie," Raven Productions, Inc. 2005, pp. 26-28.

(7). IBID, pp. 4-199.

(8). Wilderness Cookery, Charles L. Sommers Wilderness Canoe Base, Boy Scouts of America, Region 10, St. Paul, Minnesota

(9). Personal Communication with Quetico Park Headquarters Staff, Atikokan, Ontario. May, 2021.

(10). David Toop, "A Brief Review of the History of Limitation of Aircraft Over Quetico," Quetico Park Library, Dawson Trail Campground, May 5, 2021.

(11). David Olesen, A Wonderful Country..., pp 155-157.

(12). Personal Communication with Quetico Park Headquarters Staff, May 2021.

(13). Personal Communication with Curtiss Handberg from Campbell's Cabins on

Lac La Croix, Atikokan, Ontario, May 2021.

(14). Lake Names of Quetico Provincial Park, p. 8

(15). IBID, p. 32

(16). IBID, p. 23

(17). Letter From F.B. "Bill" Hubachek, Jr., September 10, 1958

(18). Public Record

(19). Letter From F.B. Bill" Hubachek, Jr. September 17, 1958.

* The first two stories in this chapter first appeared in the Winter 2019 issue of the Boundary Waters Journal. They have been revised and expanded.

Tea on the Portage

The Ojibway woman, Anwaatin(it is calm), was very sad.
Tears dripped from her eyes and moistened her face.
Her baby, Memengwaa((butterfly), was still nursing and now she had
To leave her village, her friends and family. "More space,"
Her husband, Ogichidaa(warrior), said. "We need to go to a new
Place where we have our own Weegiwahm, our own home,
Where our son, Myeengun(little wolf),can build his birch bark canoe
And grow into manhood and be free to roam
The lakes and forests where there are fewer people."

The woman stood by the canoe as her husband and son
Loaded their few belongings. She sat in the middle holding
The baby while her husband and son paddled. Everyone
In their village on Basswood watched as the canoe folded
Into the distant shoreline. A light breeze from the south
Helped to push them further along to the first portage,
To the lake where they planned to stay overnight. Smallmouth
Bass were spawning nearby, *noosa-owesi*, in the language
Of the Ojibway people.

They unloaded the canoe and started carrying their packs
Over the portage. Stopping to rest for a while
In a small clearing, father built a fire and then went back
For the canoe. Mother nursed the baby while their son piled
Up firewood. Hot tea warmed them and wild rice cakes
Satisfied their hunger. This first portage to the lake was long and uphill.
It was slow going with the baby, and even though her heart ached,
She did not complain. The second portage was easier. It was very still
As they paddled across the lake to their campsite on the point.

They were up at daybreak the next day but a heavy mist shrouded
The shoreline. They packed their gear and ate smoked venison
And tea. Soon the mist faded and they departed. Clouds
Filled the sky and it started to rain as they hastened
To the first portage where they stood under their canoe

Until the rain passed. They paddled for two days,
Always in the direction of the sunrise, until they came to
Kahshahpiwi, and as the light faded away
After sunset, they set up their camp for the night.

They rested for three days, eating fresh-caught fish, smoked bear
Meat and wild rice stew. Father was unsure which trail
To take but decided to go north through three lakes where
The Fast water spilled out of Kawnipi, sailing
Through the Forks toward Snake Falls and the lake of many sturgeons.
They portaged around the rapids and rested by a large round
Lichen-covered rock, then on to a campsite where there was a profusion
Of blueberry bushes and firewood. The next day they paddled down
Kawnipi to the village in Kawa Bay.

* This journey takes place in the late eighteen hundreds
In the area that we know today as the Quetico Provincial Park

CHAPTER FIVE

John Peyton

INTRODUCTION:

In June, 1973, my family and I moved to Duluth, Minnesota, where I joined the staff at the Duluth Clinic. It was in Duluth where we first met John Peyton. One of the first things we learned about Duluth when we moved there was the story of the I-35 freeway impasse. In essence, the original plan was to construct the freeway through downtown Duluth with a series of pillars which would elevate the freeway and which would require removing all the buildings on the south side of Michigan Street, the main thoroughfare through downtown Duluth. John Peyton had organized a group called, "Stop the Freeway," in 1970, about the same time that he opened his Lake Superior Art Gallery. John was a well-known artist in Duluth and the Lake Superior Gallery, which was located at 922 East Superior Street, was right in the path of the planned freeway.

The purpose of the "Stop the Freeway" group was not to "stop" the freeway from being built but to alert the public about the significant negative effect on Duluth if the original freeway plans were followed. Thanks to John and many others in the community, the plans were revised and a beautiful new freeway was completed in 1989.

We were impressed by two things when we visited the Gallery and met John. One was his commitment to the "Stop the Freeway" cause, to the point where we immediately joined the movement and became very active members. The second thing was his art work and his wonderful collection of paintings of the Quetico-Superior country. We were able to acquire a number of original oil and watercolor works along with lithographs and limited edition prints, all depicting scenes of the beautiful north country that we had come to love. We became good friends, and even though we moved away from Duluth in 1976, we continued to buy a few paintings. My wife and I even returned to Duluth in February, 1979, and I spent a week taking art lessons from him. He sent me a letter in August, 1983, to tell me that the highway department had finally evicted him from the Gallery. We continued to keep in touch and continued to add a few more of his paintings to our collection.

All of John's paintings that we have acquired over the years are hanging in every room of our home. They are a constant reminder of John and our great love for the Quetico-Superior country. The pictures of the paintings that are included in this book have been digitally captured by my friend, Dr. Jim Veenstra at jveegraphics.com. I hope you enjoy them as much as we do.

John Peyton photo. Photo by *The Duluth News Tribune*.

BIOGRAPHY:

John L. Peyton was born in 1907 and was 94 when he died in 2001. He was an artist and an outdoorsman before he was old enough to go to school. He was born in Proctor, Minnesota and lived in the Northland all his life. As he grew up, he traveled the lakes and rivers of the back country on his own or in the company of loggers, trappers or Native Americans. After graduating from Central High School in Duluth, he attended Phillip Exeter Academy and went on to Yale where he played on the water polo team. While attending Yale Art School and the Art Students League of New York, he studied with such masters as Charles Burchfield, Yasuo Kuniyoshi, and George Grosz. He later studied painting under Duluth artists David Erickson and Knute Helder.

John worked in watercolor, oils, pastels, and acrylics, but his favorite medium was computer generated art. "This is the freest expression of art that I have ever done, just save it and be adventurous. If I don't like the outcome I can always come back to what I just saved." His paintings and illustrations reflected his love and respect for the environment and his appreciation for the region's history. "I guess it's a fondness for the area and the wildlife and the people as well as the landscapes. Those have been the subjects of my writings and my books."

In 1970, he opened the Lake Superior Art Gallery in Duluth and gave art lessons, held art exhibits, and sold artwork from his studio. He took and active part in efforts to extend National Forest boundaries in the Wild Rivers program against the development and pollution and other environment controversies. He organized the "Stop The Freeway" movement in the 1970's, thereby helping to give Duluth the beautiful lake walk along I-35, enjoyed by residents and tourists alike.

Peyton had many stories and articles and illustrations published in *Outdoor Life, Country Gentlemen, Blue Book, Successful Farming* and many juvenile publications. For seven years he edited and published the *Magazine of Ducks and Geese* from his farm in Hermantown. He wrote and illustrated five books in his eighties. His first book, *The Stone Canoe* retells the legends of the Ojibwe and earned the 1991 Minnesota Book Award for fiction. *Voices from the Ice,* a children's book of an Ojibwe Family trip to the sugarbush was published in 1991 and *Faces in the Firelight* published in 1992 was his first novel. They were followed by his compelling autobiography, *Bright Beat the Water* in 1993 and *The Birch* in 1994.

John Peyton lived to the age of 94, and continued to write up to the end. His final manuscript, *Strife of Gods*, awaits publication. Though he was a banker, his first love was painting and nature. He revered life, family, learning and the environment. His paintings and writings are reflections of a rich and full life. "I would like to show in my paintings and books what life was like in the woods in the early part of the century. It's changed entirely since then."

John's daughter, Beryl Peyton, is keeping his work alive by producing giclee prints of the substantial holdings of original art that the family maintains. The work is being promoted through Hawk Ridge Art of Duluth. Originals and giclee prints are available in area galleries.[1]

(1): The biography of John Peyton was copied in 2012 from the Hawk Ridge web site which is no longer in service. Permission to include it in my book was given by Kris and Doug Cameron, John's granddaughter and her husband.

(all measurements are in inches)

ORIGINAL WATERCOLORS

Sailboat at rest on Lake: 10 x 14

Paddling on Saganaga: 10.5 x 13.5

Flotilla: 14.5 x 9.5

Legend of the Great Lake: 22 x 16

Spruce Tree and Open Water: 14 x 20

Tea on the Portage: 16 x 22

Loon and Island: 21 x 16

Rescue on the Ice: 16 x 11.5

Through the Ice: 15 x 21.5

Canoe on Lakeshore: 10.5 x 14

Tied to the Nets: 22 x 15

September Ridge: 14 x 11

ORIGINAL HAND PAINTED PRINTS

Over the Beaver Dam: 17.5 x 11

Canoe in Rapids: 14 x 11

Approaching the Falls: 11 x 16.5

Intruders: 9.5 x 15

Split Rock Lighthouse: 11 x 14.5

Paddling in the Rapids: 14 x 11

ORIGINAL OIL PAINTINGS

Granite Island: 23.5 x 18

Island in Lake Superior: 24 x 20

ORIGINAL PASTELS

Hunters: 16 x 21

Buffleheads: 29 x 21.5

Lady Slipper Collage: 8 x 13

ORIGINAL PEN & INK

Solo Portage: 10 x 13

PRINTS

Loon Call: 10 x 16

Fir Tree: 13.5 x 19

Log Jam: 16 x 10.5

Skidding the Log: 14.5 x 20

Branch with Beaver: 11 x 7.5

Steep Portage: 14 x 20

CHAPTER SIX

Canoeing With My Wife *

There were two seminal events in my life. The first was when I was introduced to the Quetico-Superior Country in 1956 and took my first canoe trip which I described in Chapter One. The second was in 1962 when I met my future wife, Pat, during my first year of medical school. Her introduction to the land of lakes and portages occurred during the summer of 1963. She had to take some summer courses at the University of Minnesota Duluth to finish up her nursing degree from the University of Illinois. After that she finished out the summer working as a nurse at the Ely Bloomenson Hospital. I was working as a canoe guide at Wilderness Outfitters and we used to take day trips on our days off. By the end of the summer she fell in love with the canoe country. We got married soon after that on the first day of spring, 1964, and we've never look back. We were living in Chicago at the time so when I had a three-week break from school in September, we packed up our VW Beetle and headed for Ely for a canoe trip. That first trip was the beginning of our collaboration as canoeing partners and the first of many memorable journeys into the Quetico and the BWCA. Our canoe trips brought us closer together as a couple, sharing our deep love for the canoe country and for each other. The following five trips I'm going to describe were ones that only Pat and I shared. There were many other trips we took with friends and family and many others that I took without Pat and I will relate of few of those experiences in Chapter Seven, Eight and Nine.

TRIP ONE: McINTYRE AND BRENT LAKES-1964

It had been raining in Chicago all day on the 18th of September when we finally left for Ely in the early evening. Among the personal stuff Pat insisted we pack was a large box on hair rollers, "to keep the curl in my hair." I must have loved her a lot to agree to such a request but I can honestly say that the hair rollers were never used on our trip and were never again invited on another canoe trip. We left Chicago in a heavy rain storm which finally stopped somewhere in Wisconsin. We arrived in Ely around eight o'clock the next morning, tired and hungry. After breakfast at Vertine's we picked up our gear, canoe and permits at Canoe Country Outfitters and headed out to Moose Lake to start our trip. We

![Moose Lake Campground]

Pat Dailey at Moose Lake Campground prior to the trip

were both tired from the overnight drive so we ended up camping that night at the public landing before starting our trip the next day.

I don't remember seeing many people as we paddled across Basswood on our way to our first campsite on Burke Lake. That was a memorable campsite as it was the first and only time we have ever had a bear in camp. We woke up the next morning to the sound of our pots and pans falling off the canoe where I had stacked them the night before. The bear ran away when we threw rocks and yelled at it. Apparently the reason for the bear's interest in our campsite was a big pile of trash back in the woods that I had failed to notice when we set up camp the night before. In all my years of canoeing before or since, I've never had a bear in camp.

Pat beginning the portage to Burke Lake from Bailey Bay.

We packed up and moved on to North Bay and took the beaver stream into Isabella and Side Lakes into Sarah and camped our second night in McIntyre Lake in what turned out to be our favorite campsite in the canoe country. Located at the south end of a small bay on the west side of McIntyre, I had first been there in 1956 on my first canoe trip described in Chapter One with my Uncle Jack and our guide, Mark Spink. One thing that became apparent as we made our way up the North Bay beaver stream and the portages into McIntyre, was that Pat was

Pat paddling in North Bay Beaver stream.

not only great on portages but she was also the best bowman I ever paddled with. The McIntyre campsite is unusual. The landing area is a smooth rocky shoreline about fifty yards long that slopes gently into the lake. Nestled back in the bay, it's protected from the west wind and yet allows for a nice view of sunrise. There are sites for half a dozen tents scattered among the beautiful white and red pines.

The McIntyre Creek runs along the back side of the site and is full of minnows. A little-used portage to Robinson Lake also runs alongside the creek. I camped there in 1959 with a crew of scouts from the Canoe Base and spent a day clearing the portage. It looked then like it hadn't been used for some time.

We spent the next two days in McIntyre, fishing and just enjoying the wilderness. We caught a lot of walleyes and Pat discovered she how much she enjoyed fishing. We finally broke camp and headed north, thinking we would go to Conmee. A terrific rain and wind storm caught us as we were paddling past airplane island in Brent Lake. It blew us over toward an island near the north shore of the lake. I jumped out of the canoe and held it to keep it from banging against the rocks. We waited until the storm passed and then, soaking wet, paddled around to the west end of the island where we found a campsite. It was a frightening experience for us even though we had our life vests on. The amazing thing is that Pat didn't fall apart emotionally. She said she was scared but had faith that I would take care of her. We spent the next three days in Brent drying out, resting, fishing and playing cards. We had a great time but never made it to Conmee. We stayed in Ely overnight at the end of the trip then headed back to Chicago, where I started my third year of medical school.

Pat and a stringer of fish, Brent Lake.

TRIP TWO: INCIDENT AT KAWNIPI FORKS- 1968

I graduated from medical school in 1966 and we moved to California where I spent one year as an intern at the San Bernardino County Hospital. In 1967 I entered the US Navy as a medical officer and was stationed at Camp Pendleton Marine Corps Base near Oceanside, California. By this time we also had three children, two-year old twin sons and a three-month old daughter. Since our first canoe trip together in 1964 we had talked many times about making a return trip to the Quetico. We were finally able to make it happen in July, 1968.

We flew back to St. Louis with the children and arranged for them to stay with Pat's folks. After getting everyone settled we rented a car and drove to St. Paul where we stayed overnight with my cousin, Chuck. The following day we drove to Ely, arriving there in the afternoon where we met with our outfitter Bill Rom, and made the final preparations for our trip. The next morning we headed out to Moose Lake to Rom's landing to pick up our gear, which included our new Kelty frame packs. To save paddling time we took the tow boat to Prairie Portage where we checked through customs and picked up our travel permit and fishing licenses. As we left Prairie Portage and headed for Bailey Bay we realized how much we had missed the canoe country. Being back in the Quetico was an exhilarating experience for both of us.

We camped our first night on Cigar Island in North Bay and then moved on the next day to Kahshahpiwi via Nest, Point and Side Lakes. On the third day of our 10 day trip we made it into Cub Lake where we spent a couple of days in a beautiful campsite near the Eag Creek. The fishing was very productive. Pat caught a big northern pike on a red and white daredevil while trolling one afternoon. Feeling more rested, we moved on to Eag Lake then through McDougall into Keats Lake where we had some great walleye fishing, especially below Snake Falls. In 1961, when I was guiding for Sommers Canoe Base, I had camped with a crew of scouts on "Have a Smoke Portage." We spent part of a layover day building a table from a big pine tree that had fallen down next to the portage. It was still there when we portaged into Shelley Lake on our seventh day.

It was a beautiful day, one of those special days in the canoe country when everything is just right. I paddled through Shelley while Pat cast into the shore hoping to pick up a bass or a stray northern. After we portaged into the

Kahshahpiwi Creek, she stopped fishing and helped me paddle as we were going upstream. Both of us were sitting on our life jackets. As we approached the Kawnipi Forks,[1] I mistakenly had positioned the canoe on the east side of the Creek and right into the fast water coming around the rocky point. I told Pat to paddle hard as we approached the fast water. The words were no sooner out of my mouth when the bow of the canoe suddenly shot up, throwing us out of the canoe into the water. Pat was struggling to stay up but she kept going under water. I was able to swim over to her and help her grab on to the canoe which was filled with water and floating down stream along with our packs and paddles. With her holding on, I managed to swim the canoe over to the east shore on the Creek and then went back into the water to retrieve our packs and two of our three paddles. Everything else that wasn't tied down, including out fishing gear, camera and life jackets was lost.

As you can imagine, everything was soaked and my poor wife was shivering and in shock. I dumped the water out of the canoe and told her we had to get back in the canoe and paddle over to the west shore, the other side of the creek, to avoid being swamped again. It took awhile to convince her that we had no other choice if we were to continue out trip and she reluctantly agreed. We loaded up and made it past the rushing water without incident. We found a small campsite just opposite the Forks and pulled in to dry out in the bright sunlight. As we were taking our wet clothes off, I noticed a bush with a large black sweatshirt laying on top of it that someone had apparently left there to dry. Pat put it on as she was still shivering. I laid our sleeping bags and tent on the ground to at least partially dry out. Most of our food was soaked even though they were packed in sealed plastic bags. The cheese and salami survived as did two dehydrated dinners, the peanut butter and a few Rye Crisp crackers. All of the toilet paper was ruined. It was obvious that we needed to get back to Moose Lake as quickly as possible.

After saying a prayer of thanksgiving that we had survived what could have been a real tragedy, we had a light lunch and packed everything up. We headed south to Kahshahpiwi Lake where we made camp before dark. As we paddled along we noticed that the canoe was off balance. The impact of the fast water when it hit the canoe had apparently twisted the canoe frame so we had to sit on opposite sides of our seats in order to maintain our balance. In spite of this, the next day, our eighth day, we made it all the way from Kahshahpiwi to Moose Lake just as the sun was setting, a distance of about 22 miles and 10 portages.

I discovered a number of things on this trip. First and foremost, Pat demonstrated courage in the face of adversity. She is definitely a Voyageur and she once again proved her prowess as a bowman. Second, always wear you life jacket and make sure all your gear is secured in the canoe. Third, large leaves are a poor substituted for toilet paper.

> (1): Personal Observation – We swamped at Kawnipi Forks, so named because it is the place where all the water from Kawnipi Lake pours in the Kahshahpiwi Creek on it's way west to Lac La Croix and beyond. It is a narrow area between two rocky points of land and can be treacherous. I had previously been through the Forks many times but always coming from Kawnipi, not going into Kawnipi. As far as I know, it is not named as such on any map.

> * Incident at Kawnipi Forks first appeared in the winter 2019 issue of the *Boundary Waters Journal*. It has been revised for this book.

TRIP THREE: WOODSIDE LAKE, 1970

Woodside Lake is located between Reid and Hurlburt Lakes in the Quetico. One of the guides at Sommers Canoe Base told me about what a great lake it was and that he had established a beautiful campsite on the south end of the lake. He encouraged me to go there but I never made it there during my guiding days. I told my wife, Pat, about it and it didn't take too much convincing for her to agree to go there. In September, 1970, we were living in Madison, Wisconsin, where I was doing my ear, nose and throat residency at the University of Wisconsin. I had some vacation time available so we arranged for my Aunt Bernice, who lived in Austin, Minnesota, to watch our three children while we were gone.

We planned to get to Woodside via Agnes and Silence Lakes. As we were setting up camp on our first night on Agnes near Louisa Falls, we heard heard a lot of noise and loud voices across from us. There were six canoes pulled up to the Louisa Lake portage where a bunch of guys were yelling and carrying on. We paddled over to ask them what was going on and one of the men said they were a camera crew from Alabama who were filming a movie about the Quetico.. They said they just wanted to get some pictures of the Falls and then they would be moving on to set up camp further up the lake. That's the last we saw of them or so we thought. The next day we were about two miles south of the portage into Silence when a yellow sea plane circled overhead and then landed next to us. The

first thing Pat and I thought was that something had happened to our kids. No, that wasn't the case. The guys in the plane were Canadian Rangers and they just wanted to check our fishing licenses and our travel permit.

We made it into Woodside without further incident, coming into the lake from Silence and then through a series of unmarked portages south of the lake. The campsite was just as had been described. There were at least four good tent sites, a great fireplace and was easily accessible by a gentle sloping rocky landing area. It faced north and provided good views of the sun and moon. The next day was rainy and chilly so we stayed in camp and rested. We were both in our tent when we heard a commotion near the campsite. I stepped out of the tent to find the six canoes and the group we had encountered at Louisa Falls all gathered in front of our campsite. Without so much as a "Hello and how are you?", one of the men requested that we vacate the campsite so they could move in since they had a large group and hadn't been able to find another campsite to accommodate them. I could not believe what I was hearing and I get mad even now as I write about it, 51 years later.

Well, we didn't move, much to their consternation. I watched them as they headed toward two islands on the west side of lake and assumed that's where they camped as we heard them making a racket well into the night. The next day was overcast and rainy so we decided to go fishing and were having pretty good luck with the walleyes when they suddenly showed up to do some filming. They had a bullhorn and told us we had to move as we were in their way. Mind you, this was out in the middle of the lake. We just ignored them and they eventually moved to another location. Such arrogance!

We were fixing breakfast the next morning when we saw them leaving, taking the long portage into Hurlburt Lake. We moved on the next day and made it back to Moose Lake a few days later.

TRIP FOUR – OTTERTRACK LAKE, 1982

Benny Ambrose lived on Ottertrack Lake in what is now the BWCAW, from the 1920's until his death on August 27, 1982. I knew about him when I was guiding canoe trips for Sommers Canoe Base and actually camped on Ottertrack a couple of times where he had his home but never stopped to meet him. In 1982

our family was living where we reside now, in Jacksonville, Illinois. So it was with interest when we read in our local newspaper an AP story that he had died and the U.S. Forest Service was in the process of dismantling his homestead and clearing the area to wipe out any trace of where he had lived for nearly sixty years. Pat and I decided we needed to go to Ottertrack to see his place before everything was gone. We left our four kids at home with a sitter and were on our way a couple of weeks later.

We stayed at Gunflint Lodge on September 14th, the night before starting our trip to Ottertrack, and made reservations to stay there when we returned four days later. However, before leaving the next morning, I cancelled our return reservation, thinking we could drive to Duluth and stay there rather than staying at Gunflint. That turned out to be a monumental mistake as we found out later. The next morning, September 15th, we drove over to the public landing on Sea Gull Lake, parked the car, and started out. It was a beautiful sunny fall day as we paddled our 18' Old Town Guide canoe across Sea Gull and headed west through Ogishkemuncie to Eddy Lake where we camped our first night. The next day was also sunny but cooler as we passed through Knife and Hanson Lakes then into Ester Lake and finally made it into Ottertrack in the late afternoon. We were both impressed how beautiful the portage was from Knife into Hanson. We quickly set up camp and fixed supper. It was getting chilly and Pat was tired so she stayed in camp while I paddled over to look at Benny's place which was just west of our campsite around a point and back in a little bay. There wasn't much left of the house except for a beautiful stone fireplace and chimney which was still standing, and some old snowmobiles and other junk which were parked in some tall grass along the shoreline. We stayed at Ottertrack the next day and spent some time looking around. Bennie's garden had gone to seed and the whole place looked like it was on the way to extinction.

The next day, our fourth day, was overcast and cool, and it started to rain as we packed up our gear and headed for Monument Portage and our return trip home. The wind had picked up and the rain was beating down. We tightened our life jackets and tied the packs to the canoe thwarts at the end of the Swamp Lake portage. As we passed the entrance to Cache Bay and headed into the main body of Saganaga Lake, the wind had changed direction and was blowing very hard out of the northeast on the port side of our canoe, making it very difficult to maintain an easterly heading toward the narrows at the south end of Saganaga that would take us back to where our car was parked. Pat was doing a draw stroke in the bow on the port side while was doing a sweep stroke in the stern on the starboard side trying to keep our heading into the waves at more or less a right angle. It was really tough going and we were both getting tired. We got some relief when we paddled on the lee side of Munker Island but as soon as we hit the open water again it was a battle to try to maintain our course and not swamp the canoe. Both the wind and the rain seemed to intensify and I yelled at Pat that I was about ready to give up the struggle and let the wind push us into Red Rock Bay in the southwest part of Saganaga where we could spend the night. We were not only tired but I think we were both in the early stages of hypothermia. It was just at that moment that we found ourselves very close to a small island where I was able to land the canoe. We unloaded the packs and I propped the canoe up on a low tree limb and we stood under it to get out of the rain.

We were both shivering like crazy. I had a flask of Irish whisky which we both sampled and then had enough sense to get out our Coleman stove and heat up some water for tea and eat some trail mix. We must have rested there for an hour or so and were feeling much better. The wind had died down and the rain had lightened some so we packed everything up and made it to the narrows and the public landing before dark. While we were stopped on the island to rest we talked about trying to get our reservation at Gun]flint Lodge back rather than going all the way to Duluth for the night. Unfortunately there were no openings. It turned out it was fall-color weekend in northeastern Minnesota and we ended up having to drive all the way to Minneapolis before we could find a place to stay. We were wet, tired and hungry when we finished the trip and I took a lot of deserved heat from Pat for cancelling our Gunflint reservation.

TRIP FIVE: THAT MAN LAKE – 1979 and 1984

The Man Chain of lakes in the Quetico parallels Knife lake all the way up to the lower end of Ottertrack. According to the monograph published by the Friends of Quetico Park, no one knows for sure how the lakes got their names.[1] I had guided a few crews through the Man Chain when I guided at Sommers Canoe Base. After hearing Joe Seliga tell about his weekend trips to That Man Lake (see Chapter Nine for more details), I decided that that was one place I wanted to visit again with Pat. We actually made our first trip there in July, 1979, soon after moving to Jacksonville, Illinois. We stayed two days on Joe's island campsite and then moved on to Emerald Lake and back to Moose Lake via Carp and Birch Lakes.

Our last trip there was in late September, 1984. Canoeing in the fall can be challenging as we soon found out. The sky was overcast as we paddled down Birch Lake on the way to the Carp Lake portage. It was there that we met a man who was just on his way back to Ely. He had been staying at Dorothy Molter's Isle of Pines Resort and mentioned that the resort was empty. I suggested to Pat that we visit Dorothy and stay at the resort rather than going to That Man Lake but after some discussion we decided to head to the Man Chain. We were getting tired and decided to camp in Carp and push on to That Man the next day, which we did. The weather seemed to be changing as we set up our tent on the island campsite and it was getting colder. After supper we put on our long johns and climbed into our sleeping bags to stay warm.

We hung our Coleman lantern up inside the tent to provide some reading light and some warmth. Even so it was cold. The next morning when we woke up our tent was sagging from 6 inches of snow which was covering it. Pat wasn't feeling good and sounded like she was coming down with a cold so we decided to pack everything up and head back to Moose Lake. It was really cold. We briefly entertained the idea of going to Dorothy's place when we got to the Carp Lake portage but decided to go on into Ely and a motel. Looking back we wished we had visited Dorothy instead, as the weather warmed up a few days later.

POST SCRIPT:

I have to admit that I had a kind of lackadaisical attitude regarding wearing life jackets when I was guiding at the Canoe Base. We always wore them in windy weather but on calm days we either sat on them or tied them under the canoe seats. I don't feel that way now. We never should had attempted to go across Saganaga on that windy day in September, 1982. I was so intent on getting back to the Sea Gull public landing that I ignored the wind and waves, and we almost didn't make it. The lesson to be learned is simple: if it's too windy and the white caps are rolling across the lake, pull into the shore, and don't forget to wear your life jacket.

We never kept a journal of all of our canoe trips but I wish I had done so. We took a lot of pictures but I can't find a lot of them, especially the ones of Benny's place on Ottertrack. The pictures we took on the trip where we swamped at the Kawnipi Forks were all lost. I'm not even sure how many canoe trips I've taken over the years but there have been quite a few. One thing Pat and I are thankful for is that we have passed on to our children and grandchildren our love for the Quetico and the BWCA and hope they will carry on the tradition. One great concern we have is that one day the historic battle may be lost between those of us who want to preserve this primitive wilderness area and the commercial interests who would destroy it in pursuit of financial gain.

REFERENCE:

1. *Lake Names of Quetico Provincial Park*, Friends of Quetico Park, page 1.

CHAPTER SEVEN
Canoeing with Novices

When I was growing up I loved to read stories about the old west by Zane Grey and Louis L'Amour. That's were I first encountered the term *greenhorn*. According to the Merriam-Webster dictionary the word was first used in the 15th century, referring to a young ox or bull that was "green or inexperienced." In modern usage it refers to an "inexperienced person or someone who is unacquainted with local manners or customs." The word "novice" has the same meaning. In a sense we are all greenhorns or novices the first time we do anything, like starting school or driving a car or taking our first canoe trip. I was certainly a novice when I took my first canoe trip in 1956 even though I had done some canoeing at Boy Scout camp and earned my canoeing merit badge.

From 1957 until 1963 I spent my summers working first as a canoe guide at Sommers Canoe Base on Moose Lake and then as a guide at Bill Rom's Canoe Country Outfitters and at Wilderness Outfitters. (I missed the summer of 1960 when I went to summer school.) As I look back, most of the inexperienced folks or novices I guided adjusted to the rigors of a canoe trip pretty well by the second or third day and most of them had positive things to say about their experience, even to the point of coming back for another trip. This was especially true of the scouts I guided when I worked at Sommers. Most of them had their canoeing and/or camping merit badges so they all did very well. Unfortunately this has not been true for some folks as I will describe in the following four stories.

TRIP 1: A WINDY DAY ON BASSWOOD LAKE -1963

My last year of guiding canoe trips was in 1963. In the summer of 1962 I guided for Bill Rom at Canoe Country Outfitters and was planning to return there for the 1963 season. Jim Pascoe was also working at Rom's then as a canoe trip planner along with Bob Olson and Pat Magie. Jim and I got to know each other and enjoyed a few beers at Dee's Bar on Sheridan Street. I was just finishing my first year of medical school when Jim called to tell me that he and Jim Kerntz, who owned Kerntz funeral home in Ely, had purchased Wilderness Outfitters which included Basswood Lodge. Jim Kerntz was going to manage the Lodge and Jim Pascoe was going to run the Outfitting store in Ely, which at that time was located on Chapman Street. He said he was in need of experienced help and offered me a job to work for him during the summer of 1963 to help with the outfitting and do some canoe guiding. This first story I am about to relate occurred during the summer of 1963 when I was working at Wilderness Outfitters.

A family of four had made a reservation to take a guided canoe trip during the first week in July. Jim couldn't find any guides who were free so he asked me to guide them. They had never done any canoeing before but mom and dad wanted to take a week-long trip with their two sons, ages 14 and 16. They weren't too anxious to take a paddle only trip so I suggested that we take two 17 foot Grumman double-end canoes and a 3 HP motor with a side mount which would save time and eliminate a lot of paddling. (There were no motor restrictions in either the Quetico or the BWCA at that time.) I had taken a number of motor trips with a side mount in the past and had not had any problems so I thought this would be a good option and they agreed. They wanted to stay in the BWCA so I planned our trip to start at Fall Lake, take the Basswood Lodge launch and the four-mile bus portage to Hoist Bay and then to Basswood Lodge where we would pick up our canoes and motor. From there we would motor across Basswood, down the Basswood River to Crooked Lake and set up a base camp and then return via Pipestone Bay and Newton Lake to Fall Lake. As we were loading up our gear at the Lodge, I was informed that their 14 year old son had just had ear surgery to repair a broken ear drum and was not to get the ear wet. Other than that caveat, everything was copacetic.

It was a beautiful bright warm July day when we started our trip, though a bit windy. Rather than pulling one canoe I decided to lash the canoes together side by side like a catamaran, about three feet apart, with the motor attached to the side mount in the stern of my canoe on the left along with the two boys, one in the bow and the other amidships sitting on the bottom, and mom and dad in the other canoe with most of our packs. We were all wearing our life jackets. We made good time going north from the Lodge past Washington Island and around United States Point. Just past the Point we pulled into a sandy beach campsite for lunch. The wind was much stronger now, coming out of the west but there wasn't too much wave activity.

As we passed Hansons Island and headed into the open stretch of the lake going southwest toward the bay that leads to the Basswood River, the wind really picked up and there were one to two foot white caps. Before I could turn around and head back east, the canoes started to take on water, especially my canoe where the motor was attached. The weight of the motor pulled us down and the side mount acted like a funnel for the water to come into the canoe. Within minutes, as my canoe started to fill up with water, it pulled the other canoe down enough so that it was soon filled with water and the motor was flooded. There was nothing we could do except to try to steer the canoes with our paddles as the wind pushed us in a northeasterly direction toward a group of small islands on the Canadian side of the lake.. We eventually landed on one that was about half a mile from Hansons Island.

Everything was soaked as you might imagine. We opened the packs and laid everything out on rocks and tree branches and tied some rope around a couple of trees for a clothes line. The sun was still high in the sky and with the warm wind blowing, our things quickly dried. While our gear was drying out I worked on the motor and dried it out as well. I told the family I wanted to go back to Hansons Island where there was a resort, and call Basswood Lodge to have them exchange one of our double end canoes for a square stern which I probably should have done in the first place. (I had stopped at Hanson's Resort many times in the past when I was guiding for Sommers Canoe Base and knew they had a radio phone.)

So with dad in the bow of the canoe, we started back to Hansons Island, leaving mom and the two boys to start setting up our camp. The wind was still blowing as we headed in a southeasterly direction to Hansons Island, and even though I was tacking to try to avoid another catastrophe, it happened when we were about halfway there. Again the motor side mount acted like a funnel, and water started pouring into the canoe, and the motor flooded out again. Fortunately we were able to paddle the water-filled canoe the rest of the way to Hanson's dock. I ran up to the lodge which was near the top of the island and called Jim Kerntz to tell him what had happened. Withing an hour they brought a square stern canoe from Basswood Lodge. The wind was finally dying down, and after drying out the motor again, we made it back to mom and the boys without incident. We continued on our way the next day to Wednesday Bay where we set up a base camp and made it back to Ely on time. Needless to say, because of the water-filled canoe incidents, mom and dad weren't too happy with the trip. The good news is their son did not get his ear wet.

This incident was an eye-opener for me. As mentioned earlier, I had used side mounts on canoes many times in the past without difficulty but never when there was a lot of wind and wave activity like we encountered on Basswood that day. I had violated the first rule of side mounts: they should not be used in big waves and rough water, mainly because the standard mount has a design flaw. The problem with the standard commercial side mount is that the motor mount vertical board is too close to the side of the canoe, and when water hits it, especially if it's a big wave, there's no place for the water to go except into the canoe. Having realized this simple fact of physics, I later designed and built my

Standard Old Town Canoe Motor Mount.

Notice the Old Town mounting board is less than an inch from side of canoe where it can easily funnel rough water into the canoe.

own side mount as illustrated in the accompanying pictures. My design places the motor mount vertical board six inches away from the side of the canoe. In heavy seas it is much less likely to act as a funnel. Even Bill Magie related that the same thing happened to him one time on Knife Lake[1] I don't think too many people use side mounts any more. My best advise is to avoid the big waves all together and use a square-stern canoe with your motor.

(1): Dave Olesen, *A Wonderful Country-The Quetico-Superior Stories of Bill Magie*, Raven Productions, Inc., P 174

The John Dailey designed motor mount attached to the canoe.

The Dailey designed motor mount board is at least 5 to 6 inches away from the side of the canoe thus reducing the chance water being funneled into the canoe in rough water.

TRIP 2: BWCA CANOE TRIP JULY, 1971

In 1969, after being discharged from the Navy, Pat and I and our three children moved to Madison, Wisconsin, where I started my ear, nose and throat residency at the University Hospital. We made a lot new friends in Madison and found many who shared our enthusiasm for canoeing in the Quetico and the BWCA. We also met two families who had never been on a canoe trip, but after listening to our stories about the canoe country, decided they would like to go with Pat and me and our two five-year old sons on a trip we were planning for July.

Bill was an administrator at the hospital. He and his wife, Mary Kay, had one child, Tommy, a six year old first grader. They were a very pleasant couple, especially Bill who was an enthusiastic fisherman and had had some experience camping but had never done any canoeing. Mary Kay however had no experience in the outdoors but was excited about the trip. She was a fair-skinned blond-haired lady who actually went to a hair salon before the trip and had her hair styled into a bee hive. The second family, Larry and his wife, Jean, had two children, Jane, age 8, and Bobby, age 4. They lived in a town house near us and our kids often played together. Although Larry and Jean were outdoor devotees, they did not have much experience canoeing. We met together three or four times to discuss the trip and talk about what personal gear they should take and what to expect regarding the portages and campsites. We even spent one day canoeing about 20 miles down the Wisconsin River to sharpen their canoeing skills. However it didn't seem to have made any impression on our friends once the trip started.

Our planned route was to start at Lake One and work our way around through Insula, Alice and Thomas Lakes and finish in Snowbank Lake. Pat and I realized during the first day of the trip that we may have made a mistake taking these two families on a canoe trip. From the time we started at Lake One until we got to Alice Lake, there was constant complaining about the portages and the mosquitoes and the heat and having wet feet, not from the kids but from the adults. There was also a lot of unhappiness with the trail food menu. The other problem was the weather. It was unseasonably hot and humid for the first four days until we got to our campsite on Alice, which was located on the southeast side of the lake. It had a nice sandy beach with plenty of tent sites. We cooked dinner that night and sat around talking for awhile, wondering how long the hot sultry weather was going to last when the wind started blowing and we heard thunder in the distance. The answer came abruptly in the middle of the night when we were awakened by a severe thunderstorm. Bill, Larry and I stood outside in the pouring rain, trying to divert the water away from out tents which were all sitting in about 6 inches of water. It was probably the most ferocious rain storm I have ever experienced on a canoe trip. Our air mattress were literally floating in our tent. Our sleeping bags and clothes were soaked but somehow our food packs, which were hanging up, stayed dry inside.

The next morning was beautiful: a bright sun and no humidity. We were all a bit shell-shocked from the experience but our friends were not happy, wishing they could go home. We stayed there that day and got everything dried out; the kids swam on the beach. There was a lot of tension for rest of the canoe trip which was unfortunate. We took the long portage out of Alice into Thomas Lake and found a nice campsite in Ima before moving on to Disappointment Lake for our last camp before Snowbank. When we got to the Snowbank Lake public landing. Larry and I walked back to Lake One where our cars were parked. After loading everyone up we drove to Ely to drop off the canoes and gear at the outfitter and headed for home. Things were never the same afterwords with Bill and Larry and their families.

Paddling canoe with sons Kevin and Sean, age five.

TRIP 3: BWCA CANOE TRIP 1974

When I finished my medical studies at the University of Wisconsin in 1973, we moved to Duluth, Minnesota and I joined the Duluth Clinic. Among the new folks we met, Jim and Carla stand out. Jim was a dermatologist at the Clinic. He and Carla didn't have any children but they were neat couple and we shared a lot of good times with them. They were anxious to take a canoe trip when we described our previous journeys into the bush. Neither had any camping or canoeing experience and it was with some reluctance that we agreed to take them along with us in August, 1974. Our children were older now so we hired a baby sitter who had taken care of the kids before to stay with them while we were gone for the planned eight-day trip.

We arrived in Ely around 0700 on a bright sunny August morning. The outfitter had all of our gear ready and he followed us out to the Lake One parking lot where we left our car and then took us and our gear back to Moose Lake where we took the tow up to Birch Lake. Our itinerary was to go into Knife Lake and then to Kekekabic, Ogishkemuncie, Little Saganaga and then down the Kawishiwi River to Alice and Insula and end up at Lake One. We started on a Saturday and planned tp finish up the following Saturday.

The first day went very well. After a nice visit with Dorothy Molter on the Isle of Pines and enjoying some of her root beer, we made camp up the lake near the portage into Bonnie Lake. The grumbling about the portages and the wet feet began on day two as we headed for Ogishkemuncie. We made it as far as the eastern end of Kekekabic and set up camp. Tom was wearing Levis and declared at supper that if his pant legs weren't dried off by morning he was going to cut off the wet part. The first thing I saw the next morning as we looked out of our tent was Tom walking around with his jeans cut off at knee level. We made it to Ogishkemuncie on day three and rested and fished, hoping to make it to Little Saganaga on day four, which we did. We found a nice campsite on the north end of the lake and hurriedly set up our tents as the sky was getting overcast and it felt like we were going to get some rain. The was an old metal stove from the logging days right there so we built a fire in it and positioned our rain fly over it. It still had not started raining when we settled down for the night. Pat and I fell asleep almost immediately.

I'm not sure what time the storm hit but it was one to remember. Besides the howling wind, the lightening and thunder and the pouring rain, there were trees falling all around us. We all just stayed in our tents, waiting for the storm to pass, hoping a tree wouldn't fall on us. Pat said she didn't hear the storm as she was sleeping so soundly. When we got up the next morning everything was soaked. I had tied the canoes to a tree so they wouldn't blow away and our packs were safe. It was a frightening experience for us, especially for Jim and Carla.

We decided not to move on but chose to stay an extra day in Little Sag and hopefully dry out. Jim and I went fishing in the afternoon without much success. Sitting around the campfire that night, Jim said that he and Carla had had enough of the camping trip and just wanted to get home. I explained that we still had a way to go but if we could get through a series of small lakes into the Kawishiwi River close to Joyce Lake the next day and then get through Insula to Lake Four we could certainly get back to Lake One on our eighth day.

The next day, our sixth day, we only made it to Kivaniva Lake and then struggled to the north end of Insula on our seventh day. The paddle across Insula on our eighth day was a back-breaker as we had to battle a head wind all the way to the portage into Hudson Lake. Pat and I did ok but Pat started having right shoulder pain and it may have been the beginning of a torn rotator cuff which later had to be repaired. Jim and Carla were worn out and Jim refused to go any further so we had to make camp that night in the middle of the portage. When we got up the next day, our ninth, Tom said they were determined to make it to Lake One before nightfall. In fact, we got there in the early afternoon, thus ending their wilderness experience. I have always felt bad about that trip. I just over estimated their enthusiasm and ability.

TRIP 4: BWCA CANOE TRIP AUGUST 1979:

In 1976 we moved from Duluth to Spartanburg, South Carolina, where I joined a small ENT clinic. We only stayed there for two years before moving back to Jacksonville, Illinois, where we have lived for the past 43 years. But during our brief time in South Carolina we met some great people, including our next door neighbors. Kirk and Cathy Jones and their three children, Kirk Patrick, age 10. Lisa age 12 and Catherine, age 14. Our kids all got along well and Kirk and Cathy were Bridge enthusiasts like Pat and me. When we moved back to Illinois in 1978

we kept in touch. We had told them a lot about the canoe country when we lived in Spartanburg, and even though they had never been camping or canoeing, they were excited about taking a canoe trip into the BWCA. I suppose we should have been forewarned about potential problems based on our two previous experiences related above. I promised Pat that I would pick an easy route for this trip and so in August, 1979, we met at out home in Illinois before going on to Ely. By that time I had acquired two canoes, a 17 foot Old Town Royalex and an 18 foot Old Town Guide canoe. We took two cars and stopped in Duluth for a day of sightseeing before going on to Ely. We got to Ely about noon the following day and picked up two more canoes and tents from Wilderness Outfitters and headed out to Snowbank Lake to start the trip.

In 1979 the there was a Ten Party Rule in the BWCA, meaning no more than 10 people per campsite. We had eleven in out group, five in Kirk and Cathy's family and six in the Dailey family. I knew about the rule but figured no one would bother us, especially in Snowbank, where we planned to spend our first night. By the time we were loaded and on the water it was about five o'clock and windy. I was concerned about our inexperienced group so I found a nice spot to camp on Harri Island out of the wind, except is wasn't a designated campsite. Just as we were getting camp set up a young couple in a Forest Service canoe and packing a fiberglass biffy that they planned to install somewhere, pulled into our campsite and told us that we had to move because it wasn't a designated site and there were too many of us. I told them that we were all a family and were worried about the wind. They were pretty nice about the whole thing and told us there was an unoccupied campsite near the Boot Lake portage and they would make an exception for us to all stay there one night only since it was getting late. So we packed everything up and moved to the campsite they recommended. I should have known better; not the best way to start a trip. (On the 2017 McKenzie map there are 2 designated campsites on Harri Island, one at the place where we first stopped in 1979.)

Pat and I and our kids had been on canoe trips where we had to deal with difficult portages, so the muddy, mosquito infested portages the next day as we headed for Ima Lake weren't a big deal, part of the reality on traveling in the BWCA. Our friends response was a bit different. After the campsite fiasco on day one, the mud and the mosquitos on day two were an unexpected punishment. Kirk Patrick, Lisa and Catherine struggled but didn't complain too much. However mom and dad, Kirk and Cathy, had a very difficult time. Kirk struggled mightily trying to carry the canoe and needed some help. It was at this point I think that they both wanted to go home.

After a lunch break on Jordan Lake, we finally made it to Ima. The map listed two campsites at the very southwest corner of the lake that were close together and that's where we stayed for the next four days. One campsite was on Alworth Lake, about a fifty yard walk from the Ima campsite. Actually it worked out pretty well. There was a nice place to swim in Ima and everyone gathered there for meals and evening campfires. Pat and I and all the kids stayed in the Ima campsite and Kirk and Cathy set up their tent at the Alworth campsite. For people not used to paddling a canoe, the Old Town Royalex was a real challenge. It was all fiberglass and had no keel. It was like trying to paddle a bathtub, a real bomb, somewhat like the Coleman Canoe. The three older girls, our daughter Ellen, and Lisa and Catherine were assigned to the Royalex. They struggled with it, especially in the wind. (I sold that canoe when we got back to Illinois.)

We all had a pretty good time in Ima. The kids did a lot of swimming and had fun fishing for walleyes. Pat and Cathy took off in a canoe one day by themselves and spent some time exploring. The weather was just perfect, warm and sunny. Our final campsite before returning to Snowbank was on Disappointment Lake. In some way that was was the final straw for Kirk and Cathy. It rained for the two days that we camped there and we all stayed in one campsite, taking a chance that those two canoe country cops were somewhere else. We also learned at that time one of the reasons Kirk was having such a difficult time. He was using the canoe trip to help him stop smoking, having left all his cigarettes at home. He was pretty stressed out by this time and made the comment that he had never traveled so far and spent so much money to have such a miserable time. We finally made it back to Snowbank and stayed in Ely for two more days at the Burntside Lodge before going home. Our friendship has remained intact over the years and their daughter, Lisa, actually returned in 1983 for another canoe trip.

Jones and Dailey families group picture after the trip. Photographer unknown.

Isle of Pines*

Nestled near the western end of Knife Lake,
On the Canadian border with Minnesota,
Is the Isle of Pines. "Knife Lake" Dorothy would make
Her home there from nineteen thirty until the
End of nineteen eighty-six, nearly fifty-six
Years. She lived alone most of that time,
Adopting a lifestyle that suited her, a mix
Of wilderness adventure and a new paradigm
Of social interaction. She was a beacon
Of light for all who stopped by
Her place by sled or canoe. For those seeking
Safe harbor, Dorothy's was a refuge,
If only brief, from life's deluge.

I can still see her in my mind,
Standing next to her wood-framed tent,
Her summer home. To find
Proper words to describe her slightly bent
Stature, her quiet demeanor, her subtle appeal,
Requires more than a simple comment
About her physical appearance. A grey-haired real-
Life lady who loved life, a peaceful
Woman whose kindness to all she met
Was long remembered after they left her beautiful
Island. They drank her root beer and went
On their way or maybe stayed awhile to sit
And talk. I'll remember and I won't forget.

*Known affectionately as "Knife Lake Dorothy,"
Dorothy Molter's Isle of Pines cabin was
located in the roadless wilderness area of the
BWCA, accessible only by snowmobile,
cross-country skis, snowshoes or canoe.

Original oil portrait of Dorothy Molter by John Dailey, 20" X 16"

CHAPTER EIGHT

A Family Adventure

This book not would be complete if I didn't relate the story of the canoe trip my wife and I took in June and July of 1983 with six teenagers and our dog, Emmy. This group consisted of our twin sons, Kevin and Sean age 17, their friend, Richard Bailey, also 17, our two daughters, Ellen, age 15, and her sister, Kathleen, age 11, and Ellen's friend, Lisa Jones, age 15. Kevin, Sean and Richard had just graduated from high school in June. Ellen and Lisa had just finished their freshman year in high school and Kathleen was going into sixth grade. Emmy was our feisty little Cairn Terrier.

When our children were born, Pat and I wanted to introduce them to the canoe country at an early age, hoping that they would develop the love an appreciation for the area that we had. We purchased two undeveloped lots on the south shore of Burntside Lake in 1970, about 10 miles south of Ely, when we lived in Madison, Wisconsin. We spent a lot of time camping there in the summer. That progressed into one day canoe trips and more, so by the time we went on the 1983 canoe trip that is the subject of this story, our kids had been on numerous outings into the BWCAW but had never been in the Quetico. Both Richard and Lisa had been on one previous canoe trip in the BWCA.

We moved to Jacksonville, Illinois, where we presently reside, in 1978. In April, 1983, we were hit with a terrific rain and wind storm in the early morning hours while we were sleeping. I owned two wooden canoes at that time, an Old Town 18 foot wooden Guide canoe with a fiberglass bottom that I had purchased in 1971 when we lived in Madison, and a 17 foot Seliga with a canvas bottom that I had purchased in 1980. The Seliga was stored in our garage when the storm hit but the Guide canoe had been resting on a canoe rack in our back yard. The next morning I went out to check on the canoe and it wasn't there. The wind had picked it up and carried it about 300 feet to the front yard where it was resting against a telephone pole with a couple of holes in the bottom and three broken ribs. I couldn't believe it hadn't been damaged more severely. This presented a problem in that we had made plans to take a canoe trip in June and were planning to take the Guide canoe. Coincidently, about a week before the wind storm, I had called Ralph Frese at the Chicagoland Canoe Base to order a 17 foot Old Town Canadienne canoe that Ralph had designed. I planned to use it along with the

Seliga and the Guide canoe on our June canoe trip. Luckily he had one in stock, a green fiberglass model with mahogany gunnels, ash bow and stern plates, and wooden cane seats. I told Ralph about the damage to my Guide canoe and asked if he could fix it before our upcoming trip and he said he would try. A few days later Pat and I loaded the Guide canoe on top of our car and hauled it up to Ralph. I brought the new Canadienne back home to try it out before the trip.

Ralph called the first part of June to say that he had fixed the Guide canoe and it was ready to pick up. On the morning of June 21st our group of eight packed up our two cars, my Ford Bronco and Pat's Chevy Caprice. The Seliga was loaded on the Bronco and the Canadienne on the Caprice. We left home and headed to Chicago, our destination, Ralph Frese's Chicagoland Canoe Base to pick up the Guide Canoe. This is where the story gets interesting. We didn't have cell phones back then so our plan was for Pat to follow me on I-55 north and I would lead her to the Canoe Base which was on Narragansett Avenue right off the Kennedy expressway in north Chicago. I decided to get off the Interstate at one of the exits north of Lincoln to get gas and thought she would follow me. I waited and waited but she didn't show up so I got back on the highway and got off at the next couple of exits to see if she was there but she wasn't. I was really worried and decided to just go on to the Canoe Base, hoping she would eventually show up.

What actually happened, as I found out later that day, was that she didn't see me get off the Interstate so she got off at the next exit she came to and waited for a while and when I didn't appear she decided to also go on to the Canoe Base and meet me there. When I finally arrived at the Canoe Base, she was already there and had been for an hour or so. What a relief it was to see her. We picked up the Guide canoe and lashed it next to the Seliga on the Bronco and headed for Wisconsin to our motel in Janesville. The following day we drove to Duluth where we stayed over night before heading on to Ely the next day.

We arrived in Ely in the early afternoon of June 23rd. After stopping for lunch at the A&W on Sheridan Avenue, we drove out to Tom and Woods Outfitters on Moose Lake where we planned to stay overnight before starting our trip on the 24th. Tom Ware and Woods Davis had purchased their outfitting business from my old friend, Don Beland, in 1973. (I'm still not sure why we outfitted with Tom and Woods instead of with Don who had started a new outfitting business, "Don Beland's North Country Lodge," in 1978 about half a mile east on Moose Lake.) After meeting with Tom Ware, we went over the gear we would be taking with us including 8 sleeping bags, 8 Thermarest mats, 3 tents, 3 food packs, 1 kettle pack, 1 rain tarp, 8 life jackets and 11 paddles. We also had 3 of own personal packs, a folding aluminum potty chair and our fishing gear. Most of the food we took was light weight freeze dried packs. When I checked the menu with Tom everything looked ok. It was only later that I found we had been short-changed on the food.

After getting settled in the motel rooms which were in a building next to the outfitting post, it was time for supper which was served in the dinning hall which was also next to the outfitting post. We left our dog, Emmy, in our room while we were at dinner, thinking she would be ok. When we got back to the room she was barking and had chewed up part of the carpeting. (We had to reimburse the outfitter for the damage.) The rooms were not air conditioned and it was a hot night. After breakfast the next morning we loaded our canoes and gear on 2 motor boats for a tow up to Prairie Portage where we cleared Canadian Customs and picked up our Canadian fishing licenses and Travel Permit. When the ranger noted we were going through Gardner Bay off Crooked Lake on our way north, he mentioned that there had been some problems with a couple of bears in the Gardener Bay area and warned us to be careful. Not good news.

The day was bright and sunny as we paddled out of Inlet Bay heading west for Upper Basswood Falls and Crooked Lake. We stopped for lunch at the south end of Rookery Island and continued westward past Ottawa Island and United States Point to small island just south of King Point where we camped for the first night. We immediately had a problem when we tried to set up the tents.

Kevin, Sean and Richard starting to set up first camp.

We were missing a couple of the tent poles for the Eureka tents and some fittings. We improvised but it was a harbinger of things to come. Whoever packed up the tents at the outfitters must have been asleep at the wheel or just careless. As we went along on the trip we found other things that weren't up to par such as not giving us enough packs of main course freeze dried dinners, 3 packs for 6 servings instead of 4 packs for 8 servings. We also ran out of soup mix and bread. Very frustrating. Tom and Woods seemed to be nice enough guys but the quality of their outfitting left a lot to be desired.

In his book, *Of Time and Place*, Sig Olson has a chapter about some of his favorite campsites. One of the campsites he talks about is in Bart Lake, just a short portage west of Crooked Lake, north of Wednesday Bay: "On Bart Lake an island campsite is nestled against a stand of white pines with a fireplace at the water's edge where I used to build a live box because the bass there were so plentiful."[1] After reading Sig's comments, I told Pat that we should plan to go there on this trip so Bart Lake was our destination on day 2. It took us about three hours to get our canoes and packs over Horse Portage around Upper Basswood Falls. By the time we got to Wheelbarrow Falls it was mid afternoon

Wheelbarrow Falls, Basswood River.

Lower Basswood Falls Viewed from Crooked Lake.

so we stopped for lunch before taking the portage around Lower Basswood Falls into Crooked Lake. We had to be careful to make sure everyone landed their canoes well above the falls where the portage begins on the sandy beach along the north shoreline. It was late afternoon when we stated paddling toward Wednesday Bay and past sundown when we took the short portage into Bart Lake. As we paddled north in Bart we passed an island that had a campsite but it didn't fit the description of the island campsite that Sig had described. Because it was getting dark, Pat wanted to camp there but I convinced her we should keep going to an island near the north end of Bart which was shown on the map. I had no idea if that was the island that Sig had written about. It was near dark when we got to the island but we could tell immediately that this was the place we were looking for. I hung up our two Coleman gas lanterns which provided plenty of light to set up the three tents and cook dinner. It had been a long day and everyone was tired. We were all thankful that we had found the campsite.

Our campsite turned out to be a most beautiful place in the light of day the next morning. There was a very nice sandy beach and the stand of white pines that Sig had described was still present as was the fireplace. It was very level and there were plenty of tent sites and it didn't appear to have been used very much. After a breakfast of pancakes, bacon, stewed fruit and hot chocolate, we all took time to enjoy a swim and a bath. The girls decided to sunbathe on the beach. Pat and I went exploring and fishing. The boys also went fishing. It was a leisurely day of rest for all of us. We didn't have much luck fishing but we really didn't try that hard. It was enough to spend a few hours in our island campsite and enjoy watching the clouds pass by and listen to the sounds of the wilderness.

Campfires have always been a part of every canoe trip I have taken. Gathered around a campfire at the end of the day is a special time. If only for a few brief moments our spirits are united with each other, and with our long-past ancient heritage, as we watched the flames consume the crackling wood and smell the fragrance of the smoke as it ascends into the air. As we sat around our campfire that night it was with some sadness that we decided to move the next day on the way to our ultimate goal which was Conmee Lake.

Day four also proved to be very warm and sunny. We were somewhat apprehensive as we passed through Gardner Bay where we stopped for a lunch break just before starting the series of portages into Elk Lake. We didn't encounter any bears but we were thinking about them as we unloaded the canoes to start the first short portage into a small pot hole. The next portage into Elk was much longer and confusing. There was a point in the trail where the main portage went to the left and another trail went off to the right. Unfortunately Pat and the girls took the trail to the right so when the boys and I finished the portage at Elk Lake, the girls weren't there. We found them on the other trail which kind of ended in the woods. They were sweaty, hot and angry at their predicament, and the mosquitoes added to their distress. We picked up their packs and led them back to the main trail.

Elk is a small but beautiful lake known as a great lake trout lake. We found a beautiful campsite on the north side of the lake where there was a big rock overhanging the lake which made a perfect place where one could run and jump into the lake for a swim, which all the kids did after we set up the tents. Pat and I watched them while I cooked supper, freeze dried beef stew but only six servings for our crew of eight. After lemon aid and cookies for desert we were still hungry so I popped a bucket of pop corn as we sat around the campfire after dark. My feelings of annoyance toward Tom and Woods for not packing enough food for us continued through out the trip. In fact the only member of our group who had enough food was our dog, Emmy.

We didn't have time for any lake trout fishing in Elk as we left early the next morning, hoping to get to Conmee by early afternoon. The two short portages into Cone went pretty well but we bogged down a bit on the long, muddy portage from Cone to Brent. Even so it was pretty amazing to see this group of teenagers push themselves over all the portages. Carrying the 80 pound 17 foot Seliga canvas canoe and the 75 pound 18 foot Old Town Guide canoe was no easy feat for Kevin, Sean and Richard. Pat and I paddled the 65 pound 17 foot Canadienne canoe. It was such a nice canoe, the fiberglass hull designed to glide through the water like a knife primarily because of the concave shape of the bilge at the bow and stern. I regret that I never thought to ask Ralph how he came up with idea for the design.

The paddle down Brent was made easier by a tail wind that pushed us to the portage into Conmee, arriving there around four o'clock. We found a nice campsite near the middle of the lake not far from the short portage into Suzanette. The campsite was on two levels with one of the tent sites about 15 feet above the main camp via a natural rock trail. The girls were afraid to stay up there by themselves so the boys set up their tent on the upper level and the girls stayed on the lower level with Pat and me. We did establish a latrine on the upper level and positioned the folding potty chair there. Emmy stayed with Pat and me as she couldn't make it up the trail to the upper level.

We stayed in Conmee the following day fishing for walleyes and whatever else we could catch. Richard caught a couple of nice northerns which we released but mainly we had great success catching walleyes. It was a good feeling to be back in Conmee which has always been one of my favorite lakes in the Quetico. There is something about the lake other than the fishing that draws one back. Our campsite didn't lend itself to swimming in the dark, almost mysterious waters of Conmee, so other than brushing our teeth and washing our hands and faces, no one went swimming. Other than the girls hiding the guy's underwear while they were out fishing, our time in Conmee was uneventful.

Ellen, Lisa and Kathleen reading in camp by lantern light.

We left Conmee on June 30th, our seventh day and took advantage again of the predominantly westerly wind as moved down Brent and then across McIntyre to the portage into Sarah. My first encounter with that portage was when I was guiding for Sommers Canoe Base in 1958. It seemed almost insurmountable, especially when going uphill from Sarah to McIntyre. The secret is you have to go up (or down) using the protruding rocks for footholds, winding your way back and forth while maintaining your balance. It was about noon when we got to Sarah. After a quick lunch break we decided to push to on to North Bay of Basswood via Side and Isabella. For some reason our son, Sean, stepped on the stern cane seat in the Guide canoe, resulting in hole in the seat. (We were able to remove the seat at the end of the trip and leave it with Joe Seliga to repair.)

![Resting around Johns Island campfire, Basswood Lake. Photo by Sean Dailey.]

Resting around Johns Island campfire, Basswood Lake. Photo by Sean Dailey.

It was late afternoon when we set up our last camp on Johns Island in North Bay. The kids set up the tents and gathered firewood while Pat and I fixed supper. We all sat around the campfire after we ate and talked about our trip. Kathleen, our 11 year, old had left to go to the potty which was back in the woods. We suddenly heard her screaming and she ran back to where we were gathered, very upset. She said a large animal with horns had come upon her as she was sitting on the potty chair and that's when she screamed and came running back to the campfire. I went back in the woods to investigate but didn't see anything unusual. Kathleen said she thought it was a moose. I'm still not sure what she saw but it definitely scared her.

We made it back to Moose Lake by late afternoon the next day, Friday July 1st. We had to paddle against a headwind almost all the way back from Prairie Portage.

It was a real struggle. I had Kathleen paddle in the bow of my canoe. She did a great job but complained of groin pain when we finally got back to Moose. (We discovered she had developed an inguinal hernia when we got back to Jacksonville; she had to have surgery a few weeks later.) I was pretty upset with Tom and Woods about the problems we had with the tents and not having enough food. They apologized and so forth but they didn't reduce the outfitting price. We stayed in their motel rooms that night and left the next morning. We stopped in Ely to say hello to our friend, Joe Seliga, and asked it he would fix the broken cane seat, which he agreed to do. Then we headed for Superior, Wisconsin where we had reservations at a hotel on Barkers Island. The Old Town Guide canoe and the Seliga were tied down to the Bronco which I was driving and the Canadienne was lashed to Pat's Caprice. It was at this point in our journey, when we got to Superior, that an unusual incident occurred.

Superior is separated from Duluth, Minnesota by the St. Louis River, which is a tributary of Lake Superior. The two cities are connected by the John A. Blatnik High Bridge, the second longest bridge in Minnesota. Our family had lived in Duluth for three and a half years years from 1973 to 1976 and really enjoyed our life there so when we moved away Pat and I and the kids left a lot of friends behind. We still kept in touch with a lot of them and always enjoyed coming back for a visit. When we got to our hotel, someone suggested that we go to a movie that night in Duluth at the theater which was located near Miller Hill Mall. Our son, Sean, said that he had a good friend when he was in grade school in Duluth, Rosemary Knoedler, who lived on Vermillion Ave in Duluth and wondered if we could invite her to go to the movie with us which we all agreed would be fine. So he called her and she accepted his invitation. I was a little concerned about driving around Duluth with the canoes on the cars but there was no safe place to store them.

Our plan was for me to take the three girls in the Bronco and drive to Rosemary's home with Pat and the boys in her car following behind me. Then after picking up Rosemary we would all go the movie theater. I remember checking the tie down ropes on the canoes on the Bronco but I didn't check the ones on Pat's car. I was ready to leave but there was some delay with the boys so I decided to go on ahead and when Pat got the boys loaded she would follow. It took about 20 minutes to get to Rosemary's house. She was ready to go and I said that Pat and the boys would be right behind me. After waiting for an hour or so I was getting very worried but she finally arrived and explained what had happened. As she was going over the High Bridge, the Canadienne had slipped off her car and bounced a few times on the bridge pavement. Fortunately, there were two men in the car following her and they stopped to help the boys put the canoe back on top of her car. Aside from a few scratches the canoe was not damaged, which was a miracle. The only explanation for what happened is that someone may have loosened the ropes while the car was in the parking lot. I was at fault for not checking the tie downs as I had on the Bronco. I think Pat suffered the most from the shock of seeing the canoe falling off the car. Even though we arrived late, everyone enjoyed the movie and Sean said it was nice to see Rosemary again.

We left Superior the next morning, and drove as far as Janesville, Wisconsin. Because it was the fourth of July weekend, it was slow going, especially as we got close to Chicago. We got around Chicago with out any problems on Monday, July 4th, and were heading south on I-55 by Boiling Brook when we had our final unusual incident occur. There were pieces of wood on the highway and Pat ran over them and immediately got two flat tires on the Caprice. There were nails in the wood and that did the trick. One tire was completely flat and the other was about half way gone. We replaced the totally flat tire with the spare and drove about a mile or so to the next exit where there was a Shell station. I'm not sure why but we ended up buying four new tires. By the time we left there is was about 8 pm and by the time we got back to Jacksonville it was after midnight.

Epilogue:

Looking back now at that canoe trip, which was almost 40 years ago, Pat and I are so happy we had that opportunity to be with our kids and Lisa and Richard. It sure would have been a lot easier in many ways if we had had cell phones. It was an adventure from the time we left home until we returned. Tom and Woods are long gone, having sold the business in 1994. Kevin and Sean and Ellen and Kathleen all have children and Ellen and Kathleen are grandmothers. Emmy has passed on and we still miss her. I later sold the Canadienne canoe to a friend who still has it and I gave the Seliga canoe to my son, Kevin, and the Old Town Guide canoe to my other son, Sean.

(1). Sigurd F. Olson, "Of Time and Place," Alford A. Knopf, New York, 1952, pg.76

CHAPTER NINE

October Surprise*
Canoeing with the Wind, Ice and Snow in the BWCA

Dateline: 31 December, 2006, Big Lake, Minnesota

As I am writing this story I'm sitting here in a small cabin located on the shoreline of Big Lake, about 20 miles north of Ely just off the Echo Trail. This story is about a canoe trip three of my friends and I experienced about three months ago in October, 2006. Looking out of the window there is a heavy snow falling, even more of a reminder of our trip. One difference is the air is very still, so you can almost hear the snow falling as it covers everything like thick white frosting. The snow fall we experienced in October was not still and peaceful.

This is a story of survival, of how four very experienced middle-aged men survived a surprise snow storm and partial freeze up in the Boundary Waters Canoe Area. Even though it was a dangerous situation, the severity of which none of us had experienced before on a canoe trip, there are a number of reasons why we survived without incident. First and most important, we didn't panic. We also had plenty of warm clothes and were assured that we had enough food for a few extra days. We all learned a long time ago that we are not in control when dealing with the wind, rain, heat and cold, and in this case, snow and ice. One of the most important lessons to learn about wilderness survival is that you have to adapt. You have to respect nature and become a part of it. That's the great challenge and reward that awaits us each time we venture forth into the woods and leave civilization behind.

All of us were looking forward to our canoe trip with great anticipation. Tom, Bill and Chuck and I had been on a number of canoe trips together over the years, always in the fall of the year. We were all experienced in the ways of the canoe country, at least we thought we were until this trip. It all started on the afternoon of October 6th. Tom and I traveled from our homes in central Illinois and met Bill at his home in River Falls, Wisconsin, about midnight. We added his gear to ours and then headed to St. Paul to pick up Chuck. We continued on through the night, arriving in Ely in the early morning hours of October 7th. After a brief stop at Wilderness Outfitters where we picked up our fishing licenses, camping permit

and a few last minute items, we drove out to the public landing at Snowbank Lake where we parked the car and the canoe trailer. Chuck and I were in my 16' Old Town Canadienne, (not the same one mentioned in Chapter eight) a fiberglass model designed by Ralph Freese, and Tom and Bill were in Tom's 17' fiberglass wooden canoe that Tom had built. We were pretty well loaded down with extra winter clothes, just in case the weather changed and it got colder. We had heard before we left home that there might be a cold front moving into our area so we wanted to be prepared. Chuck was in charge of taking care of the food for this trip as he had done on previous trips, and he assured us he had plenty of grub. (In retrospect I think Chuck underestimated what we would need.)

By the time we got the canoes loaded and started paddling, we encountered a mild headwind. We didn't know it then of course but that headwind was just the beginning of a long week of paddling into the wind with the added hassle of snow and ice. Having driven all night to get to Ely, we were tired and decided to set up camp our first night in Disappointment Lake and then move on the next day to Thomas Lake if possible. Our ultimate goal was to get into Alice and Adams Lakes and then back to Snowbank via Kekekabic, Vera and Ensign Lakes. We were all hoping to get into some walleye, lake trout and northern fishing.

Our second day, October the 8th, was sunny but cool and very windy, especially in the afternoon. In fact, as I was unloading my canoe at the end of a portage into a pothole before the portage into Jordan Lake, the wind literally lifted the canoe off my shoulders as I was unloading it and carried it about fifteen feet before setting it down. Other than a couple of scratches it was ok but it was a harbinger of things to come. Our progress that day was also slower than usual because of low water at the beginning and end of some of the portages. We had to muck our way up to the portages rather than paddle up to them as we would normally do. That fact would also prove to be a problem for us later in the trip. By the time we got into Jordan, paddling against a head wind in the main part of the lake, we decided to make camp early and do some fishing. We didn't catch any fish but Chuck fixed a great meal and we enjoyed a dram of Irish whiskey before turning in for the night.

October 9th, our third day, started out sunny and calm. There was no wind as we started out, hoping to make it to Alice Lake. We had an easy paddle across Ima Lake. The water level in the mile-long beaver stream that connects Ima with Thomas Lake was very low near the three east-end portages close to Thomas

Lake, necessitating walking along side the canoes and pushing and pulling them. When we finally made it to Thomas, the wind was blowing out of the east. By the time we made it to the southeast end of Thomas it was late afternoon so we decided to stop for the day and push on into Alice the next day. Once again, low water had slowed us down. We were also concerned because the weather seemed to be changing with a steady wind blowing now out of the northeast and the temperature was dropping.

The realization that the focus of our trip had changed was apparent the next morning, October 10th, our fourth day. The wind had blown steadily through the night and continued through out the day. It had also changed direction. Our campsite was located at the south end of an island which did not afford much protection from the wind which was now blowing out of the northwest. We saw two canoes off to the south going with the wind heading for Kiana Lake. That was the last time we saw anyone until the end of the trip. We couldn't use the canoes to fish because of the wind so we tried casting from the shoreline. It was too windy to build a fire in the designated area so we set up two tarps to try and block the wind and we used our gas stoves for cooking. We passed the time by hiking around the island and resting in our tents. As nightfall approached we cooked an early supper and then climbed into our sleeping bags to stay warm. Earlier in the day I had gotten my boots wet so I left them outside the tent when I turned in. It was hard to fall asleep because of the howling wind through out the night.

When we awoke the next morning, October 11th, our fifth day, the landscape had changed dramatically. It was as of the wicked witch from the north had visited us during the night. The ground and our tents and canoes had been dusted with a layer of snow. The water in our buckets was frozen as were my boots. The intensity of the wind seemed to be increasing and it was very cold. After a hasty breakfast of coffee and oatmeal prepared on our Coleman stoves we moved back into the woods to get away from the wind and to try to figure out what to do. With the wind now coming directly out of the west, it was impossible to paddle back the way we had come in and we were reluctant to push further east into Alice and Adams where we would still eventually have to contend with the west wind as we paddled back toward Snowbank. Our original plan was to return to Snowbank on October 14th, our eighth day, but unless there was a dramatic change in the weather, we were virtually stuck on our island. There happened to be another smaller campsite on the east side of the island so we hiked over

Our canoes dusted with snow and snow on the ground, October 11, 2006, day five.

there and built a fire in the grate to warm up. We stayed there most of the day and cooked an early supper before heading back to our wind-blown tents for the night. I'm not sure why we didn't move to the smaller campsite which was more protected from the wind. All we could do was to wait and hope the storm would break up and the wind would calm down enough for us to paddle back the way we had come which was the shortest way home. Our main concern with paddling into the wind across the open waters of Thomas and Ima was the possibility of swamping the canoes in the middle of the lake and dying from hypothermia. Even though we were all experienced paddlers we had a deep respect for the vagaries of Mother Nature.

On October 12th, our sixth day, our situation looked even bleaker than the day before. As I opened the tent flap, snow was blowing all around us and the wind velocity had increased significantly. In fact it was too windy to use our wind-protected gas stoves so we picked everything up and found a small clearing back in the woods where we set up the wind tarps and moved some dead logs into place that we could sit on. Our supply of white gas was getting low, forcing us to cut back on using the stoves. Fortunately there was a lot of dead wood nearby so we built a campfire and kept it going throughout the day. Chuck also discovered that he had only brought a limited supply of cocoa and dry soup mix, so we drank a lot of hot tea and coffee and made a watery chicken vegetable soup to keep warm. It kept snowing most of the day and by the time we finally gave up and went to bed there was an accumulation of six inches of snow on the ground.

Wintery Day on Thomas Lake, October 12, 2006, day six. Huddled back in the woods away from the wind, cooking soup, John, Tom and Bill. Photo by Chuck Mertensotto.

The wind kept blowing through the night. The next day, October 13th, out seventh day, we spent most of the time sitting around our campfire in the woods drinking tea and coffee and the watery soup trying to stay warm and out of the wind, Our food supplies were dwindling away, in spite of Chuck's assurances at the beginning of the trip that we had plenty of food, and the Irish whiskey was gone. We just wanted to get home and so we decided that if the wind subsided, even a little, we would pack up the next morning and start back. We even thought we might be able to make it to Snowbank in one day.

We were up at first light the next morning, October 14th, our eighth day. The wind was still blowing out of the west but less than the previous few days. Everything was frozen that was outside the tent and our canoes were covered with a blanket of snow. We were so anxious to get going before the wind picked up that we skipped breakfast and just packed everything up. Even though we were still facing a headwind as we paddled away from our campsite, it wasn't as bad as we thought it might be until we rounded the narrows on the west side of Thomas to paddle across the last mile to the portage that would take us into the beaver stream to Ima. The sun was behind us and the wind was blowing into our faces. Chuck and I kept up a steady pace, never resting until we were near the shoreline for fear the wind might turn us sideways if we stopped paddling. I know our Guardian Angels were there with us. We did have a bit of a problem locating the portage at first as everything on the shore was covered with snow.

Now we faced a new problem. We had gotten an early start and had made it across Thomas unscathed. We trampled through the snow and ice over the first portage to a small pothole. A short paddle took us to another snow-covered portage into the beaver stream that would lead us shortly to the portage into Ima. This is where we encountered an unexpected and frustrating problem. The water was low and the stream was covered with a layer of ice for about 6 yards from the end of the portage but fortunately the ice was thin and we were able to break it up with our paddles. About 100 yards further on we encountered the next short portage. At the end of that portage the ice was at least a inch thick and it extended about 50 yards from the portage. We loaded our canoes and tried the same technique of breaking the ice with our paddles but it was too thick. Finally we tied a long rope on the bow of my fiberglass canoe, and with both Chuck and me on board, Bill pulled the canoe up onto the ice and the weight of the canoe broke the ice. I remembered seeing pictures of ice breakers in the Arctic doing

Breaking the ice on beaver stream from Thomas Lake to Ima, October 14, 2006, day eight.

the same thing. It worked just fine but it really slowed us down. Tom paddled along behind us where we had opened the path, picking up Bill when we broke free of the ice where the water was deeper. We finally got to the portage into Ima about noon and stopped to fix lunch before going over the portage. We were able to remove some of our outer clothes as the sun was overhead and provided some much needed warmth.

Tom was the first to start the portage and Bill and I followed, leaving Chuck behind to close up the food pack. As I neared the end of the portage I heard the wind blowing and noticed that Tom had set his canoe along the side of the trail rather than putting it in the water to start loading. I flipped my canoe down next to his and looked out at the lake. There were white caps streaming across the lake and the wind was blowing hard out of the west, pushing the rough water right into the end of the portage. Any attempt to launch our canoes and paddle into that headwind would be a real mistake, and dangerous. There was nothing we could do now but wait until the wind died down, hopefully before dark, so we could find a campsite somewhere on Ima. We did not want to set up camp at the end of the portage where we were stuck.

After carrying all the gear over the portage we found a flat area back up the trail and pushed the snow away so we could put down our tarps to sit on. Tom pulled out his sleeping bag and took a nap while the rest of us set up the stoves and made a pot of tea and some watery soup. Chuck sliced an onion, tossed in some cabbage and squash, and added the rest of our summer sausage to make a stir fry. It tasted great but there wasn't nearly enough of it. Our food supplies were just about gone. Chuck surprised us by serving a few cookies that he had in his food pack, the first we had on the trip.

Our last campsite, Ima Lake, breaking camp at sunrise, October 15, 2006, day nine, six inches of snow on the ground.

It was almost dark except for the red glow in the western sky. The wind had abated enough that we were able to load the canoes and head due west toward the portage into Jordan Lake. On the south side of the shore near where the Jordan river starts we found a campsite. The landing area was a rocky shelf which was covered with snow and ice and was very slippery. Using our flashlights for illumination, we cleared about 8 inches of snow from a flat area and set up one tent for the four of us. We were packed in there like sardines but we were warm. However, it was difficult to sleep between the snoring and frequent trips outside the tent to relieve full bladders.

We woke up to a beautiful sunrise on October 15th, our ninth day, everyone hoping that we would make it back to Snowbank by the end of the day. The air was clear and calm but very cold. We packed up and were soon in Jordan where we took a snack break before leaving Jordan to portage into Adventure Lake. The portage out of Jordan was very icy in places and snow-covered. Because of the low water level, we encountered a large sheet of ice on the water at the end of the portage but we were able to break through it without too much trouble. We then had a very short portage into a beaver stream that led into Adventure Lake. The beaver stream was covered with a two inch layer of ice that extended at least 100 yards from the end of the portage. It was too thin to walk on and too thick to break up with our paddles. There was no way we could walk around it as the ground around the edge of the pond was mushy and we sank in over our boots when we tried to walk on it. Our only hope was to somehow break up the ice like we did the day before with the weight of the canoe. But that method wasn't possible because there was no way we could pull the canoe over the ice because we had no way to walk ahead of the canoe to pull it. We finally solved the problem by putting some packs in the bow of my fiberglass canoe for extra weight and then sliding the canoe onto the ice bow first, with Tom sitting in the stern. As he pushed the canoe forward, the heavy bow smashed the ice and then he using his paddle to help break the ice piece by piece, making an ice-free

Breaking the thick ice on the beaver pond going into Adventure Lake, October 15, 2006 day nine. John, on the left, and Chuck, watching Tom break the ice. Photo by Bill Lorenzen.

path through which we could paddle into the lake. We made it across Adventure and into Jitterbug and Ahsub though we had trouble locating the portage from Ahsub into Disappointment Lake because of the snow. We finally made it back to the public landing on Snowbank by mid afternoon, again fighting a head wind across Snowbank As you might imagine, our wives were worried about us because we were a day late. One of them contacted the sheriff who was in the process of sending out a rescue party when we showed up.

John and Bill at Bill's home in River Falls, Wisconsin, after the trip, October 17, 2006. Photo by Donna Lorenzen.

We left Ely later that afternoon, tired but happy to have survived the ordeal. Getting back a day late was much better than not getting back at all. We later heard about two people who were out canoeing on a lake near Ely that same week who drowned when their canoe capsized in the wind. I know that none of us will ever forget the trip. We also decided there would be no more late fall canoe trips because the weather is so unpredictable. We were frustrated that our fishing trip turned out to be an unexpected challenge to survive but we came through it unscathed. An old friend of mine, Don Beland, former canoe guide and outfitter told me he survived a near-death experience when he swamped his canoe in some rapids in the Atikokan River during the 1964 Atikokan to Ely canoe race when his foot got caught in some deep underwater rocks. The rapids were supposed to have been marked but they weren't. Reflecting on the experience he he said most people don't die, they kill themselves by taking unnecessary chances. Instead of paddling through the rapids he would have portaged around them had they been properly marked. Another well-known canoe guide, outfitter and author, Sigurd F. Olson, said the same thing in a different way in the introduction to his book, *The Lonely Land*:

> "There were no heroics in our travels and we took few chances, believing that desperate adventures were the result of lack of knowledge and foolhardiness."[1]

We learn from our mistakes and we can avoid mistakes by learning from those who have gone before us.

(1) Olson, Sigurd F. *The Lonely Land*, 1961, Alfred A. Knopf, New York, pg. 19

* This article was originally published in the fall, 2016 issue of "The Boundary Waters Journal." It has been modified and expanded from the original.

CHAPTER TEN*

Six Canoe Country Men Who Influenced My Life

Nothing stays the same, things are always changing, and there's not much we can do the stop it. It's a bit unnerving. All of the men I'm going to tell you about have passed on. I miss them and many others who I won't mention. They all influenced my life in a very positive way. It's hard to believe that I've gotten old and don't have too many, if any, canoe trips left in me. I have developed arthritis in my right wrist, probably from doing the J-stroke a few thousand times, and my footing on the portages isn't the best anymore. My heart and kidneys and my left hip are also a problem. Carrying packs like I used to just isn't possible anymore. I used to be able to carry my 100 pound Old Town wooden canoe and my personal pack over most of the portages non-stop, but not now. Such is life. I hope to be able to tell you a little bit about each of these men who helped make it possible. All of them, in one way or another, by sharing their deep feelings for the canoe country, had a profound positive effect on me, and I thank them for that.

Mark Spink paddling his canoe. Photo from Spink family archives.

MARK SPINK

My introduction to the Quetico-Superior Wilderness area was in July, 1956, when I took my first canoe trip with my dad, my uncle Jack and two cousins. We outfitted at Bill Rom's Canoe Country Outfitters for a ten-day trip into the Quetico. My dad wanted to take a guide with us and Bill recommended Ralph Marcus 'Mark' Spink, a suntanned, balding, lean six foot tall fellow who changed my life. Mark was a seasoned canoe guide. He started guiding at Sommers Canoe Base on Moose Lake in about 1946 when he mustered out of the Army Air Corps, and was guiding canoe trips for Bill Rom in the summer of 1956 when I first met him.

Mark was the perfect guide for our group, his cool demeanor often functioned as a foil between my dad and my

uncle who frequently disagreed on how things should be done, like washing the dishes in hot soapy water or just wiping them off in cold water as my uncle was used to doing. Mark was well organized and he knew the lay of the land, and had a great collection of stories which he shared with us, often quoting a few lines from Shakespeare. The thing that impressed me most about Mark was his great love for the canoe country. I was so captivated by the whole canoe trip experience that I told Mark that I wanted to be a guide like him. Since I was involved with scouting, he said the best way to get started as a guide would be to work at Sommers Boy Scout Canoe Base on Moose Lake as he had done. He promised me he would write a letter of recommendation for me to the Boy Scout Region Ten office in St. Paul. As a result I received a letter from the Canoe Base offering me a job during the summer of 1957 as a swamper, which I will explain later.

Mark and I kept in touch over the years though I'm not sure how long he continued guiding. I met him once in 1958 on the Kekekabic portage but never saw him again on the trail by the time I stopped guiding in 1963. He joined the faculty of Western Michigan University in Kalamazoo in 1966 and retired in 1989 as a Professor of Media Services. He produced a number of movies that won critical acclaim including one titled, *Joe Seliga: Canoe Builder*, and another one about the Quetico titled, *Return*. He called me to tell me about the Seliga movie and sent me a copy. It's a wonderful record of Joe building one of his beautiful wooden canoes.

The last time I saw Mark was in July, 1990, when we met in Kalamazoo after he had retired from WMU. I later sent him a copy of an article I had written for the *Boundary Waters Journal* in 1988 about the trip I took around Hunter Island in 1958 and which is reproduced in Chapter Three of this book. He sent me a nice letter in return and gave me directions to his home where we planned to meet but never did. He said one thing in his letter that I want to share and which I agree with completely:

> "Those of us who share the north country experience, on much more than a superficial level, are bonded in special ways."

Mark and his wife later moved to Colorado. I received one or two letters from him but we never saw each other again. He died in 2002. It was because of Mark that I began a life-long love affair with the canoe country and I shall be forever grateful to him.

HENRY BRADELICH

Henry Bradelich with John on Sommers Canoe Base landing, Moose Lake, 1975. photo by Pat Dailey.

The Swamper Program at Sommers Canoe Base was a month-long training session designed to evaluate and train young men who desired to be canoe guides at the Base. One prerequisite was you had to be active in Scouting and hopefully an Eagle Scout. I didn't qualify for the latter as I still needed a few merit badges for Eagle, but I was enthusiastic about Scouting and really wanted to be a canoe guide. It was here that I first encountered my friend, Henry Bradelich, in July, 1957.

Henry was the assistant Base director and was in charge of the first half of the Swamper training program which involved two weeks of manual labor around the Base. There were two other swampers in training when I arrived, Jay Poole from Meadville, Pennsylvania, and Barry Bain from Del Rio, Texas. The three of us were kept busy from dawn to dusk completing Henry's "projects." The second half of our training involved going on a canoe trip with one of the senior guides who we were assigned to by the Guide Chief, Dave Ziegenhagen.

Henry was dedicated to Sommers Canoe Base. Although he lived in Eveleth, Minnesota, and was a teacher and counselor in the Eveleth schools in the off season, it was apparent that the Canoe Base was his number one squeeze. In addition to being our straw boss during the day, he spent time each evening telling us about the history of the Base and the canoe country, going back to the French Voyageurs and up to the present day. He especially liked to tell us stories about some of the guides who had preceded us. One of his favorites was about the two guides who paddled from the Base on Moose Lake to North Bay of

Basswood then up the Silence-Shade route to Agnes and then back to the Base via Agnes, Sunday and Bailey Bay in one day. Not being familiar with any of those lakes at that time, I really didn't appreciate what a feat it was, if in fact, it really happened. But it did affect me, whether it happened or not, for it was during this time that I started thinking of myself as a modern day French Voyageur. With his wire rim glasses and soft-spoken voice he gave the appearance of a mild-mannered easy going sort of guy and to a certain extent he was. In actual fact he was tough and demanding and his strength of character inspired a whole generation of teen-age greenhorns like me who aspired to be wilderness canoe guides.

Henry was still working at the Base in September, 1975, when I stopped by with my wife and two sons. I borrowed a Grumman Canoe from the Base, compliments of Henry, to go along with our Old Town guide canoe for a trip to the Quetico. That's the last time I saw him. He hadn't changed much. He retired from teaching in 1976. He was 86 when he died in 2001.

RON WALLS

Ron Walls was from Bartlesville, Oklahoma, and was an Eagle scout as were most of the guides. He was eighteen when I met him, just a year older than me. And yet, he looked a lot older as I remember him, with his beard and voyageur physique, medium stature, broad shoulders, energetic and a great sense of humor. However he wasn't opposed to growling at you if you did something stupid.

After two weeks of working with Henry, I was assigned to accompany Ron who was to guide a crew of scouts from Cleveland, Ohio. I had met Ron during my time of manual labor and was impressed by his no nonsense approach to guiding: evaluate the group you're going to guide and help them plan a trip they can complete. Ninety percent of the scouts who signed up for a canoe trip at the Base had no real understanding of a wilderness canoe trip

Ron Walls 1957 canoe trip.

so the guide had to help the crew make the right choice as to what kind of trip they would take: easy, moderately difficult or challenging. This particular group consisted of ten scouts and were accompanied by two dads. With Ron and me, there were fourteen of us which meant four Seliga wooden canoes and the Old Town wooden canoe that I had picked out. They were big kids who were up for a challenge so Ron accommodated them.

The canoe trips at that time were eight and a half days, returning to the Base the afternoon of the ninth day. Our first day was a long haul. We spent the first night of our trip camped in lower Agnes Lake, near Louisa Falls. I was pooped and wondered if I could hold up for the entire trip. The next day we camped in McKenzie Bay in Kawnipi Lake. Day three was a layover day to rest and fish and then on to the western end of Sturgeon Lake where we also spent day five. On day six we went down the Maligne River to Tanner Lake and then over the long, wet and muddy Tanner portage into the Darky River and then into Darky Lake, or Darkwater Lake as it's now called. On day seven we picked up a tailwind on Brent Lake and sailed across Brent and McIntyre using our rain tarps for sails and camped on Bear Island in Sarah Lake. On our eighth day, we moved on to Bailey Bay in Basswood where we camped on the sandy beach campsite. We discovered a giant pile of tin cans which we dumped in the lake, following the Park Ranger's recommendations at the time. Our trip ended in Moose Lake in the early afternoon of our ninth day.

After the trip Ron recommended me for a guiding job the following season. I learned a lot on that trip with Ron that made a lasting impression on me for the rest of my guiding days. He was a top-notch guide. Unfortunately I didn't see much of Ron after that and I lost track of him after the 1961 season when I stopped guiding at the Canoe Base, The thing I remember most about Ron was his passion and respect for the canoe country. I ran into Ron again in 1970. We had bought some property on Burntside Lake and Ron, who had a law practice in Ely and was also the City Attorney, handled the legal part of the sale for us.

1978 was a tumultuous year for northeastern Minnesota with the lingering controversy over the ultimate status of the Boundary Waters Canoe Area (BWCA) following the Wilderness Act of 1964. The details of the situation are all recorded in the 1995 book by Proescholdt, Rapson and Heinselman, *Troubled Waters*. There was pressure from the Federal Government to try to resolve the question of motorboats, logging and snowmobile use in the BWCA. In essence, if

the local authorities didn't resolve the problem, the bureaucrats in Washington would and neither the Friends, the environmentalists nor the Alliance, those who opposed the wilderness designation, wanted that to happen. So Ron was chosen by the Alliance to meet with Chuck Dayton, at shrewd environmental attorney, who represented the Friends, to come up with a compromise agreement that would satisfy everyone. The end result was the famous 1978 Dayton-Walls compromise agreement for the BWCA that amended the 1964 Wilderness Act and resolved, at least for a time, the lakes where motorboats could be used, banned all logging and limited snowmobile use.

Neither side was happy with the compromise, and Ron endured a lot of criticism from the Alliance, in spite of the fact that it was a no-win situation. Two years later, Ron retired from his law practice and moved to the Twin Cities. But he made history and will always be remembered as a man who loved boundary waters and did his best to resolve an unresolvable dilemma. He died in 2004.

SIGURD F. OLSON

I met Sig Olson for the first time when I returned to the Canoe Base in June, 1958, to begin my first year as a canoe guide. He had been invited to the Base for a number of years to give a talk to the staff prior to the start of each season. Sig's wife, Elizabeth, accompanied him on this particular occasion and I also met her. We gathered together for dinner in the historic lodge that had been built by Finnish carpenters in 1941. After dinner, Sig gave an inspiring talk about the history of the canoe country, encouraging all of us to help in the ongoing battle to preserve the boundary waters wilderness. Having been a canoe guide and an outfitter when he was younger, he shared some of his adventures and his great love and devotion for the Quetico-Superior country. His words, expressed in his soft-spoken manner, were just what I needed at that time to help me to realize what a great opportunity I had been given to be part of this wilderness area. He also mentioned that he had recently published a book, *The Singing Wilderness*, in which he expressed in greater detail his thoughts about the canoe country. I bought a copy of the book later that summer and read every chapter over and over. I still have that copy minus the dust jacket. Mine is a 1957 fifth printing issue. I looked for a number of years for a 1956 first edition back in the 1970's and 1980's without success. In 1986 I even wrote to Elizabeth thinking she might know where I could find a first edition. She sent me a very sweet

Sigurd Olson. Photo from Listening Point Foundation archives.

letter telling about how much she and Sig enjoyed meeting the staff at the Canoe Base. She also mentioned that the Canoe Base presented Sig with a paddle that had a loon in flight painted on the blade and just when the presentation was made, "a loon flew overhead and called one of the most melodious calls – it was a moment." Unfortunately she could not help me out with a first edition copy of *The Singing Wilderness*. (Recently I have seen signed, first edition copies of the book advertised on line, selling for $300.00.)

Sig talked about his son, Sig Jr, who was with the Fish and Wildlife Service in Alaska. He mentioned that jobs were available in the summer as stream guards, during the salmon run. I thought it might be an interesting job so I wrote to Sig in December, 1958, to see if he could help me get a job in Alaska the following summer. He wrote back to me in February, 1959, to console me about not getting the job but hoped that I would be returning to the Canoe Base for another summer of guiding. He also asked me to stop by to see him in June as he was making plans to do a survey job in South America that would start in July. Unfortunately, I didn't stop by to see him and he didn't make it to the Canoe Base for his talk in 1959. Although I never saw him again in person, we traded letters over the years.

I was looking through my November, 1980, issue of the *Audubon* magazine and found an article about Sig titled, "Leave it to the Bourgeois." There's a picture of Sig on page thirty-three sitting at his desk in front of his typewriter smoking his pipe. I wrote a letter to him telling him how much I enjoyed the article and reminded him about the time when we first met at the Canoe Base in 1958. He wrote back to me a few days later, recalling the time in 1958 as the "golden days" and how much the Canoe Base guides inspired him. He said he thought the *Audubon* article was "well balanced and very fair as to outlook." He liked..."the illustrations," especially "...the one where I am sitting at my desk with the smoke curling up from my pipe, just as I am sitting right now." He also mentioned that he doubted I could find first edition copies of any of his books.

Whenever I think about Sig I am reminded of the Bible verse, John4:44, "...a prophet hath no honor in his own country." He was often vilified for his work to preserve the Boundary Waters and his efforts in that respect did have a negative economic on a lot of good people at the time. That was unfortunate and an unintended consequence of preserving this magnificent wilderness for generations to come. His book, *Reflections From the North Country,* was published in 1976. When he signed my first edition copy he wrote the following note inside the front cover:

> This book embraces my wilderness philosophy reached after many years of searching here in the Quetico-Superior and all over the Northwest Territory of Canada clear up to the Arctic Coast, the Yukon and Alaska. I know you will understand it for you too love the wilderness and its deeper meaning.
>
> Warmest Regards, Sig

Sig died unexpectedly in 1982. I used to subscribe to the *Ely Echo* and was surprised and sad to read Jim Vickery's piece in the January 18, 1892 edition that Sig had passed away "...while snowshoeing near his home in Ely."

JOE SELIGA

Joe Seliga was a master wooden canoe builder who lived and worked in Ely. I first heard about Joe in 1957 when I started working at Sommers Canoe Base. At that time the only canoes that the Base had were wooden ones, seventeen-foot Seligas and seventeen-foot Old Towns. The Seliga canoes all had fiberglass covered bottoms and the Old Towns had canvas covered bottoms. Both canoes were heavy, averaging about 80 to 100 pounds as compared to the aluminum canoes that are about 70 pounds and the Kevlar and graphite canoes in use today that weigh about 40 pounds. The following year, 1958, my first year as a canoe guide, the Base purchased about 60 seventeen-foot Grumman aluminum canoes and that was the beginning of the end of the wooden canoes at the Base. But that was also the beginning of my friendship with Joe. The first time I met him was in 1958 at his shop which was in his garage behind his house on Pattison Street in Ely. I helped deliver a couple of old fiberglass Seliga Canoes that the Base had that needed some major repairs. Even though they were being phased out, there were still some Seligas that were in use in 1961.

Joe Seliga was a unique individual. He was a joyful man who was not only a master canoe builder but a friend to all who met him. He inspired me not only by his gentle nature and his craftsmanship in designing and building canoes but also by his many stories, especially the ones about his exploits in the Quetico. My favorite was the one that involved Joe and his friends who worked with him in the mines. They were all avid walleye fishermen. The Man Chain, and specifically That Man Lake, was a frequent destination. Joe related how on some Friday afternoons after getting off work at the mine, the guys would collect their gear and head to Moose Lake. They would load up their square-stern canoes and motor up to Birch Lake, then take the short portage into Carp Lake and finally portage into That Man Lake. They had a favorite island campsite where they usually camped and even left some of their stuff there over the summer so they wouldn't have to haul so much gear each time. Those were the days when the only permit you needed to go anywhere in the boundary waters or the Quetico was a fishing license. On Sunday afternoon they headed back to Ely and were ready for work on Monday morning. Joe said they always caught a lot of fish. Interestingly enough, after hearing Joe's story that campsite became a favorite of my wife and me whenever we made it to the Man Chain. That's where we were camped when we experienced a six inch snowfall that I related in a story earlier in Chapter Six.

Joe Seliga with the last canoe he built.
Photo by Deborah Sussex.

In 1980 I purchased my first Seliga, a beautiful seventeen-foot wooden craft with a canvas bottom and mahogany gunnels. I acquired my second canoe

from Joe in 1984. We used both of these canoes on a number of family canoe trips. A few years ago I gave one of them to my oldest grandson and one to one of my sons who gave it to his son. In 1987, I found what was left of a sixteen-foot canoe that had been stashed away in a lumber yard shed in my home town. It had been built by the St. Louis Boat and Canoe Company sometime in the 1940's. All that was left was the wooden frame, the gunnels, a couple of thwarts and the bow deck on which was imprinted the St. Louis Boat Company name. It was literally about to fall apart. I called Joe and told him about it and asked if he could restore it. He said if I could get it to him he would take a look at it. I built a wooden frame out of 2 x4's to stabilize the canoe and later that summer hauled it up to Ely on top of my car. When Joe looked at it he thought he could restore it and he did a beautiful job. I never used it on a canoe trip. I tried it on a small lake near my home and brought it back to Ely a year of two later and donated it to Sommers Canoe Base.

My wife, Pat, and my kids all met Joe and his wife, Nora. On more that one occasion when we stopped by to say "hello," we were treated to coffee and sweets with them in their kitchen. My friend, Mark Spink was a good friend of Joe, as well as a professional movie producer. He made a wonderful movie, referred to earlier, over a period of two weeks or so showing Joe building on of his canoes from start to finish.

There is also a beautiful book about Joe, *The Art of the Canoe with Joe Seliga*, written by Jerry Stelmok that includes great photographs by Deborah Sussex. I was so fortunate to have known Joe, and like everyone who knew him, miss him. He died at age 94 in December, 2005.

DON BELAND

I first met Don Beland in the summer of 1962 when I was guiding canoe trips at Bill Rom's Canoe Country Outfitters. I had heard about Don who was known as an excellent canoe guide and fisherman. So it was quite a surprise when Bill told me he wanted me to partner with Don on a guiding job. Two business men from Chicago wanted to go on a canoe trip with their ten-year old sons, and each dad wanted a guide. Because they were short on time and wanted to catch some fish, Don suggested going to Crooked Lake and use square-stern canoes, each with a three hp motor. We started the trip by taking a tow from Moose Lake to Prairie

Portage and then motored across Basswood to Upper Basswood Falls.

At that time in my career I had not had much experience using square-stern canoes with motors though I had had a lot of experience with my dad's 18 foot wooden John boat with a 25 hp Evinrude in the Mississippi River near my home in Illinois. The trip with Don was a teaching experience for me and here's where it gets interesting. Don's philosophy was similar to the Indians referred to by Sig Olson in his book, *The Lonely Land* , *"...Indians never carried a foot further than they had to. If they could approach within a hairbreadth of the lip of a chute, they would..." Rather* than taking the mile-long Horse Portage around Upper Basswood Falls, we took a series of short portages where we had each father and son walk along the portage while we paddled the canoes downstream to the next big rapids. Just before the canoe got to the rapids we put the motor back in the water, started it up, and motored over to where they met us. Then we short-portaged everything around the rapids and did the same thing again, paddling the canoes to the next rapids until we completed the entire portage. Don did it first to show me how it was done and said, "...don't wait too long before you start the motor..." I never did tell Don that it scared the crap out of me. What if the motor wouldn't start? Well, it's not for the faint of heart and of course you can't do it now anyway because motors are not allowed in the Basswood River. We did the same thing in reverse at the end of the trip.

I learned a lot from Don on that trip to Crooked Lake, especially observing some of his fishing techniques. He was a real professional. My primary job on the trip was to set up camp and do the cooking while he took on the responsibility of catching fish, and he was very successful. As a guide at Sommers Canoe Base, I was mainly concerned with teaching the scouts the fundamentals of wilderness canoe camping. Fishing was of secondary importance, so I never really learned the secret of canoe country fishing until I met Don, though in spite of Don's tutoring, I never considered myself a good fisherman. Later that summer Don paired up with my old buddy from the Canoe Base, Barry Bain, for the first International Canoe Derby, a race from Fall Lake near Ely to French Lake at the northern edge of the Quetico and then back to Fall Lake. I was there at Fall Lake when the race started one afternoon in July, 1962. The whole story about the race, as described by Don, is in the Fall 1989 issue of *The Boundary Waters Journal.* It's a must read.

Later in 1962, Don established his own outfitting business on Moose Lake. When

my wife and I and our kids moved to Madison, Wisconsin, in 1969, I contacted Don and he outfitted us on a couple of trips before he sold the business in 1973. He later opened a new outfitting business in 1978 at the old Anderson's Resort on Moose Lake, "Don Beland's Wilderness Canoe Trips and North Country Lodge."

The main lodge was a dark-colored log cabin and there were bunk houses for the canoe parties to stay in before and after the trip, as well as cabins along the lake for folks who wanted to just relax away from home. I outfitted with Don at his new place a number of times. One time in particular stands out. In August, 1986, one of my sons, Sean, my cousin, Chuck, my brother-in-law, Ted, and four other friends from home set out on a ten-day trip to the Quetico. Only three of us had been on a canoe trip before but it turned out to be a great trip. We camped our first night on North Bay then went up the Silence-Shade route to Agnes and Kawnipi where we rested for a day before moving up the Wawiag to Mack Lake and into Cullen Lake.

Don Beland sitting on his front porch, 2016.

I remember we had some trouble finding the portage from Mack into Munro. After a layover in Cullen where we didn't catch any fish, we made it back home to Moose Lake via Saganagons and the Man Chain. Aside from having trouble sleeping because of a chorus of snorers, everything was fine until the very end when our food supplies ran low and we got stranded for a few hours on the Birch Lake portage because someone forgot to pick us up.

Don finally gave up the outfitting business in 1994 and concentrated full-time on sled dog racing with his wife, Val. She was a gold medal international champion musher and the two of them raced their dogs all over North America. I used to follow their exploits in the local Ely newspaper, The *Ely Echo*, each week during the season. I didn't know that Don had become a master knife maker until I read Stuart Osthoff's Boundary Waters Journal article about Don in the Fall 2015 issue. I called Don and talked to him and Val. It had been a long time since I had seen either of them and was particularly interested in finding out more about

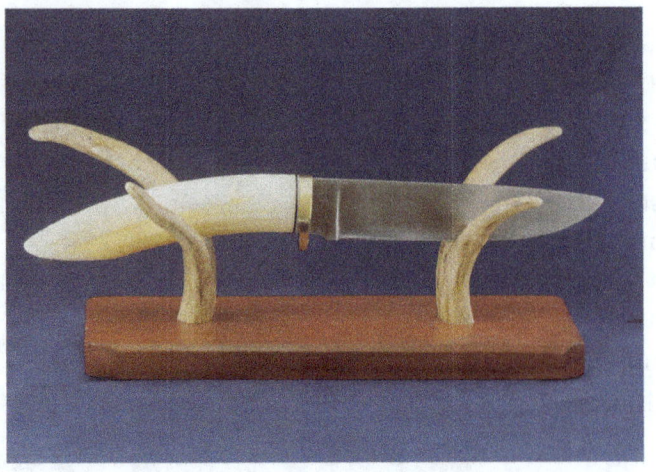

An original Don Beland knife, made 1/10/19 The Ivory handle is carved from a Hippopotamus tooth with a high carbon steel blade. The deer antler stand was also made by Don. Photo by Jim Veenstra.

his knives. My wife and I made a trip to Minneapolis at the end of October that year to the St. Paul Fairgrounds where Don was exhibiting his knives. The knives were really spectacular. I think I bought eight or nine knives at that time and since then I've bought eight or nine more. I've given most of them away to family members and friends but I still have six or seven that I keep in a display case and one in my truck. We later visited Don and Val at their home outside of Ely in September, 2016. In addition to showing us all their sled dog racing trophies, Don took me through the whole process of knife making in his shop. He was pretty impressive for a man in his eighties doing such fine work. One could write a whole book about "Don the Knife Maker." Don and I have kept in touch by phone since then. The last time I talked to Don and Val was in early September, 2021, when I called to check some dates for this article. So it was with shock and sadness when Val called me on October 6th to tell me that Don had passed away on October 4, 2021. I feel privileged to have known him all these years. He was a good friend. He also liked my poetry book, *The Portage Trail and Other Journeys*, which I published in 2019.

*This story was previously published in the winter 2020 issue of the Boundary Waters Journal. It has been revised and expanded for this book.

Don and Val Beland in their Ely home, September, 2016, Some of Don's knives are on the wall behind them.

Wilderness Symphony

He first heard it in the canoe country up north.
He listened to the music, my old
Friend, Sig Olson, as he set forth
On his many trips into the woods. He told
Us he could hear a symphony of sounds:
The wind rustling the branches of the pines
And water rushing along as it pounds
Against the shore in a storm. The sign
That all is well when the haunting trill
Of the loons cavorting in the lake
Remind us that we are home again. The thrill
Of being here again in our wilderness escape,
The singing wilderness.

How does one describe the symphony,
The music of the wilderness,
Wherever it may be? It's not a cacophony
Of sound. It's more like a peaceful stillness.
Music that envelopes one and soothes
Life's burdens, cares and woes.
It is the absence of noise, whose
Presence ruins the equanimity that flows
From the tranquility of the quiet sound
Of silence. Most of the world has never heard
This symphony of which we speak nor found
The peacefulness they seek nor heard the words,
Of the singing wilderness.

CHAPTER ELEVEN
My Last Canoe Trip – August 2015

My last canoe trip took place in August, 2015, marking my sixtieth year of canoeing in the Quetico and the BWCA. I was accompanied by my oldest grandson, Sean Michael Dailey, his friend Connor Blanquart, our guide Zach Imes and Lyra, Zach's beautiful English Cocker spaniel. Sean and Connor were recent college graduates and both had taken time off from work for the canoe trip. Sean had a steady girlfriend at the time with the prospect of getting engaged and married in the near future. I was getting older and wanted to take one more trip with him before his responsibilities as a newly-wed took precedence.

Getting ready for a canoe trip into the Quetico and/or BWCA always takes a lot of preparation. It's not something you can just decide you want to do and then pack up and head up north. Not like in the so-called "old days" which Joe Seliga talked about in Chapter Ten, when you could drive up to the lake with your canoe and gear and start paddling or motoring off on your trip. You really only needed a fishing license.

Sean and I started planning in May for our canoe trip in August. We both wanted to go back to the Quetico where we had fond memories of our trip to Kawnipi in 2008. On that trip Joe Sadaj, a younger grandson and Sean's cousin, our mutual friend, Milo Persic, and our guide, Zach Imes (and Lyra), rounded off our group of five. Aside from the fact that I had my usual problems sleeping at night, it was a great trip. We had plenty of walleye fishing and a beautiful island campsite near McKenzie Bay.

We talked about going back to Kawnipi, and initially, planned to get there by going via Carp Lake and then up the Man Chain to Saganagons and the Falls Chain. But after thinking it over, I told Sean I wanted to back to Conmee one more time where it all started for me in 1956, as noted in Chapter One. We soon found out the price of going to the Quetico had increased a lot since 2008. By the time we got our Remote Border Crossing Permit from Canadian Customs and our Quetico Travel Permit for our ten-day trip for four adults and our fishing licenses, we had spent about $1200.00.

Since Sean and Connor both had jobs we agreed to split the cost of the outfitting and travel fees and I would pay for the guide, Zach. We did a complete outfitting package with my friend, Gary Gotchnik, at Wilderness Outfitters, which is now out of business. It was just easier for me as I had given away all of my camping equipment, including my canoes. The best investment I made was to have our friend, Zach, along as our guide again to help get everything organized. I actually started traveling with a guide in 2005, which was my grandson Sean's second trip. I was tired of being the "guide." Having a guide along worked our well in 2005 and on our 2008 trip to Kawnipi.

Sean and Connor drove up to my home in Jacksonville, Illinois, from St. Louis, arriving about 0400, on August 14th. We loaded all our fishing gear and personal items into my Ford F-150 and headed for Ely, arriving there about 5 PM that afternoon. It was hot even for Ely. We met with Zach and had dinner at Sir G's Italian restaurant, a tradition before each canoe trip. (My wife and I have been going there since 1974 when it was first opened by Victor Gozzi. It was originally on the west side of Sheridan Street but moved to its present location when Bernie Hutar closed the KFC and bought Vertines, which was located at the corner of Sheridan and 2nd street.) After dinner we headed back to the bunk house across the street from Wilderness Outfitters where we spent a warm restless night. We were up for breakfast at Britton's Cafe at 0600 the next morning before putting all our packs in the Wilderness Van and drove out to Moose Lake to the public landing where we loaded everything in the boat that was to haul us and our gear to Back Bay of Basswood Lake via Prairie Portage. It saved us a lot of paddling time.

We portaged from Back Bay into Pipestone Bay and then paddled to the mile-long Horse Portage around Upper Basswood Falls where a lot of the old Hamms Beer advertisements were filmed by Les Blacklock in the 1960's. (I outfitted Les on one of his trips when I was working at Wilderness Outfitters in 1963.)

After taking a lunch break, we started over the portage. The day was very hot and sunny and as I started down the trail with a pack sack, the fishing rod case and a couple of paddles, I started to sweat profusely. I felt myself getting overheated and had to stop numerous times to rest before I finally made it to the end of the portage. I was too weak to go back for a second load even though I was drinking a lot of water. I just didn't feel good. I had never experienced anything like that before. Sean, Connor and Zach all had to made two trips.

Sean Micheal Dailey, my grandson, in the bow at the portage into Crooked Lake from Greer Lake.

Everyone was pretty spent and the heat didn't help. We finally made it to our first camp in Crooked Lake later that day after taking a short cut through Greer Lake and avoiding Wheelbarrow Falls and Lower Basswood Falls.

Washing dishes after supper, Elk Lake.

I don't remember much about that first camp. Still not feeling well, I helped set up my tent and went to bed, avoiding much supper except for drinking a lot of water and some Kool Aid. I felt a lot better the next morning and we were soon on our way, Sean and I in one of the Kevlar canoes and Connor and Zach in the other. We stopped for lunch in Gardner Bay and then portaged into Elk Lake where we planned to stay for a couple of days. It was still hot and sunny but we seemed to have adapted as we all felt pretty good. We stayed in

a very nice campsite on the north side of the lake where I had stayed with my wife and kids on a trip in 1983. There's a nice rock from which you can jump into the water to swim which was great for the kids. We caught of few walleye and a couple of nice lake trout which we released but decided on day four to move on to our ultimate goal which was Conmee Lake.

Morning mist on Elk Lake.

The temperature had fallen to the low 70's as we made our way over the long portage from Cone to Brent and stayed sunny as we paddled north on Brent to the portage into William Lake, thinking we might spend a night there before moving on to Conmee. However, the sky started to cloud over and there was some wind out of the west when we got to William. We took a brief lunch break and starting looking for a campsite as we moved northeasterly across the lake toward Conmee but didn't see anything that looked promising. As we finished portaging into Conmee a light rain started to fall. I noticed I was a little unsteady walking on the portage and again seemed to get fatigued easily, very unusual for me. Sean and Zach insisted I take it easy on the portages after Horse Portage on the first day so I usually only made one trip.

We found a nice campsite on an island on the south side of Conmee and after setting up camp, caught some walleyes for dinner. It started raining later that night and continued to rain intermittently for the next two days. We continued to catch walleyes but the rainy cloudy weather was a bit depressing. Before starting the trip, my wife and my grandson insisted I take along a folding cot to sleep on instead of a Thermarest sleeping pad, hoping I guess that I would sleep better. Well, it didn't work. I usually had to get up three or four times during the night to pass water, and trying to get out of my sleeping bag and off the six inch high cot and then back on it again and back into my sleeping bag was a major task, and it didn't help tromping around on the wet ground in the dark.

Sean and John on Conmee Lake campsite. Photo by Zach Imes.

One of the things I wanted to do in Conmee was to go back and check the Flat Rock Island campsite where we stayed on my first canoe trip in 1956. I had looked at it on our 1983 trip and it was pretty run down then and it was the same in 2015. It didn't look like anyone had been camping there for a long time. We also spent some time fishing in the same place where I caught the big northern in 1956 but came up empty-handed. It rained pretty hard at times on our second full day on Conmee so we didn't do much fishing. Our Bialetti Espresso Maker got a quite a workout as we sat around the campfire under the rain tarp and Zach prepared some great meals, especially the baked and fried walleyes. We also enjoyed the vodka lemon aid drinks the Connor prepared each evening throughout the trip, being careful that the vodka lasted to the end.

Cooking a Walleye dinner, Conmee Lake campsite.

Connor, Zach and John, Sarah Lake campsite photo Sean Dailey.

Most of our gear was still damp as we packed up on day seven to leave Conmee. It was overcast but gradually cleared by the time we got to the narrows in McIntyre where there is a beautiful campsite where we stopped for lunch. The island is covered with norways and white pines with a blanket of pine needles covering the ground. After lunch, we pushed on to Sarah where found a neat campsite in the narrows between the east shore and the large island, not too far from the portage into Side Lake. There was a nice breeze so we hung all of out wet stuff up to dry out before setting up the tents. I was feeling pretty good by now. I had had no problem paddling throughout the trip, just the unsteadiness walking on the portages. I was particularly impressed with Sean and how he handled himself. For example, the portage from William Lake to Conmee starts out on a collection of large rocks which you have to carefully maneuver over before you get to the actual trail. He just jumped on the rocks, threw on a pack and the canoe and took off. I used to be able to do that. The portage out of Conmee to Brent starts out on a 40 degree rock face which can be slippery when wet. It didn't seem to bother him as he loaded up his pack and the canoe and went up the rock face like a mountain goat.

The next morning, day eight of our trip, we broke camp early and headed for the portage to Side Lake. It was here where we met the first person we had seen since our first day on the Basswood River. She was a very nice lady who looked to be about fifty, traveling by herself with her dog, a couple of packs and a fifteen foot kevlar canoe. She must have been camped in Sarah as she was heading in the same direction as we were except when she got to Side Lake she turned north, heading for Kahshahpiwi. She said she was from Thunder Bay, Ontario, and this was her second trip of the summer. I never thought to ask her where she had started her trip to wind up in Sarah but the route back to French Lake or Lac La Croix would be challenging if either place were her starting point.

We camped our last night, day eight, in Burke Lake, battling a headwind across North Bay and all the way to our campsite on the south end of Burke. We arrived in Inlet Bay of Basswood about 10 AM the next morning. Our motorboat tow from Prairie Portage back to Moose Lake was scheduled for 1 PM so we had some time to spare. Never having explored the eastern part of Inlet Bay where the long portage to Poacher Lake begins, we paddled over and found a beautiful sandy beach where we landed the canoes and fixed lunch. The sandy beach extended inland a bit and we found a little-used campsite. It was a very restful place, away from constant canoe traffic over Prairie Portage.

Canoe on sandy beach, Inlet Bay, Basswood Lakeshore.

We made it back to Ely later that afternoon. After checking our gear in at the outfitters and taking a shower, we all headed over to the Ely Steakhouse on Sheridan Street for dinner. We agreed it had been a good trip from many perspectives. While we didn't catch a lot of fish, fishing wasn't our goal on this trip though we did have some nice walleye dinners thanks to Zach who did all the cooking. It was Connor's first canoe trip. He adapted pretty well to the lifestyle of the voyageur though I couldn't convince him to not chop or split fire wood while wearing his flip flops. Sean Michael did very well and has learned to paddle and handle the portaging with his pack and canoe like a pro. Not long after the canoe trip, in June 2016, he and his fiancee, Amanda, got married. He now has three beautiful children and I hope someday when they are older he will introduce them to canoe country. After two canoe trips with Zach he has not only been our guide but has also become a friend. He reminds me of my first guide, Mark Spink, who I have written about in Chapter one and Chapter ten. Zack is easy going and well organized and we were fortunate to have had him with us. We were also privileged to have Lyra, Zach's traveling companion. Not only did she protect us from wild squirrels and chipmunks who tried to invade our campsites but she also stood guard at night scaring off the mosquitos and bugs with her fearsome appearance. Zach told me recently that she has passed away. Very sad. She was a sweetheart.

Lyra, Zach's dog, an English Cocker Spaniel, and our fellow traveler on my last canoe trip.

I didn't realize it at the time but for me it was really a trip of remembrance, especially going back to Conmee, one of my favorite lakes in the Quetico. Even though I have a lot of emotional ties to Conmee, I can't say it's my favorite lake because I like all the lakes. Each lake in the Quetico and the BWCA has its own special quality though overall I prefer the lakes in the Quetico.

We left Ely very early the next morning on August 24 for the long drive back to Illinois. We stopped in Duluth to look at the house where I used to live back in the 1970's on East Superior Street then headed over the Blatnik high bridge to Superior, Wisconsin and south to Jacksonville, Illinois where we arrived in the late afternoon.

Wilderness Day

I heard the water softly lapping
Up against the rocky shore and sensed
The gentle breeze upon my face as I lay napping
'Neath the fading sunlight, and all was still.

The sky above so pure and blue
With scattered clouds like white cotton,
The only sound, the wind blowing thru
The branches of the giant pines around my tent.

How can I capture the feeling of that day?
The sense of contentment that all is well,
And if it were possible, I'd rather stay
Here in the wilderness forever.

CHAPTER TWELVE

Final Thoughts

Taking a canoe trip into the BWCAW or the Quetico Park has always been for me an exciting experience and hopefully that's the case for most folks. In order to make it a great experience, proper preparation is very important. Here I'm talking about not only being in shape physically for the rigors of canoe tripping but knowing something about the territory. Reading about the area makes the trip a whole lot more interesting. The canoe country is a very historic place and the more you know about it will make your trip more rewarding. A great source of information about the BWCAW and the Quetico is available in the writings of Sig Olson. I would especially recommend his first book, *The Singing Wilderness*. It contains some great chapters that beautifully convey Sig's wilderness philosophy. *The Voyageur, The Voyageur's Highway* and *Rainy River Country*, by Grace Lee Nute, published by the Minnesota Historical Society, all provide excellent historical information about the area. *Plants of Quetico and the Ontario Shield*, by Shan Walshe, is a loaded with information about the flora of the canoe country. *The Boundary Waters Journal*, published by Michele and Stuart Osthoff, is a wonderful source of current information about fishing, camping, equipment and more. The magazine is published four times a year and well worth the nominal price for a subscription. As Meredith Wilson noted in his Broadway Play, *The Music Man*, "You've got to know the territory."

I did mention a number of different canoes that we've used over the years. My first canoe was an Old Town wooden canoe with a canvas covered bottom. I used it all the time that I was guiding at Sommers Canoe Base. It was very heavy by today's standards. It weighed about 80 pounds at the beginning of the season when the canvas was dry from being stored over the winter but picked up 20 pounds of water by the end of the summer. When I started guiding for Bill Rom and Wilderness Outfitters in 1992 and 1993 we used Grumman Aluminum canoes. They weighed less but didn't handled as well as my Old Town.

I purchased an Old Town 18 foot wooden guide canoe with a fiberglass bottom in 1971 when I lived in Madison, Wisconsin. It was a good canoe but heavy for portaging. I later gave that canoe to my son, Sean, who still has it. Sometime around 1977 we took a family trip to Maine and visited the Old Town Canoe

Company in Old Town, Maine. I picked up an Old Town Royalex canoe that was on sale. It was rigged for double duty as a sail boat with detachable side boards and a mast and sail. I never did use it for sailing but it was one of the worst canoes I ever had for paddling. It had no keel and paddled like a bath tub, kind of like the infamous Coleman fiberglass canoe, which also paddled like a bath tub. It was very difficult to handle in the wind.

The 17 foot Seliga wooden canoes with the canvas bottom are fine canoes and great for paddling plus they were made by my friend, Joe Seliga. They are beautiful seaworthy crafts that handle very well in rough water and are easy to paddle. Their only downfall was they weigh about 80 pounds. I could carry one when I was younger but not now. The 17 foot fiberglass Old Town Canadienne is also an excellent canoe. Designed by Ralph Frese and weighing about 60 pounds, it has beautiful lines and handles great in any kind of weather. Light-weight kevlar canoes are the canoes of choice now days. They are certainly easier to carry over the portages. I know Stuart Osthoff is a great fan of the Northstar aramid/carbon fiber canoe as he has reported in the BWJ.

With regard to canoe paddles, I would avoid the fiberglass/carbon or the aluminum paddles. I prefer a well-made wooden paddle with a nice wide blade such as the Bending Branches Expedition paddle also recommended by Stuart Osthoff. Having the right paddle is just as important as having the right canoe.

When buying a paddle you have to choose between the straight shaft paddle and the bent shaft paddle. There are pros and cons for each type. I have used both straight shaft and bent shaft paddles and I prefer the latter. When I paddle, which is usually in the stern, I use different strokes and I think the bent shaft is more efficient. The J-stroke is used most often to keep the canoe going in a straight line to complement the bowman's draw stroke. I also use a draw stroke where I pull the paddle straight back along the side of the canoe and sometimes a sweep stroke which also helps to correct the direction of the canoe. (What stroke you use depends on which way the wind is blowing.) I also like to switch sides and paddle on both sides of the canoe rather than paddling on the same side all the time. When I switch sides the bowman also changes sides. It allows the shoulder and arms muscles on one side to rest when I switch sides, again increasing efficiency.

Just a brief word about portages. Having the right mental attitude about portages makes them much easier. After a long paddle, getting out of the canoe and walking on a trail through the woods can sometimes be the best part of the trip. Take your time and enjoy the opportunity to follow the paths that may have been traveled by native Americans and French voyageurs before you.

Which brings up the question of what kind of shoes are best for canoeing. I personally have always worn ankle-high boots with good vibram soles. Investing in a good pair of boots will give one good footing and ankle support and will make walking the portages easier and safer. I would avoid non-slip sandals, flip flops, crocks and sandals. In 2011 my grandson and I walked part of the Camino de Santiago in Spain. Parts of the trail were pretty rough and I was happy that I had good fitting ankle-high boots.

When I started working at Sommers Canoe Base in 1967, one of the first things I was taught was that most of the portages have rocky landings, and rocks and canoes don't mix well. To protect the canoes at those times it was often necessary to stand in the water next to the portage and carefully unload the packs and gear from the canoe and not let the canoe bump up against the rocks. That means you have to get your feet wet.

Now some people try to avoid the wet feet by wearing rubber boots that are about knee high. My friend Stu Osthoff, has figured out a way to unload the canoe and keep his feet dry. Personally it doesn't bother me to get wet feet as long as the canoe is safe. I just change into my dry non-slip sandals when I get to camp. I must admit that when my wife and I were canoeing, I made every effort to help her keep her feet dry when we came to a portage.

As far as pack sacks, cooking gear, tents and sleeping bags, my only comment is that most of the stuff available today is much improved from what we used in the fifties and sixties. Two items that I would recommend for sure are the Coleman single burner gas stove and the small Coleman gas lantern. We used to carry two of each on almost every trip. What kind of food you take, freeze dried or fresh, depends on how much weight you want to carry.

When I started tripping with my friends Bill Lorenzen and Tom Wilson around 2000, I learned something new about personal hygiene. Up to that point

whenever I took a bath on a canoe trip it involved jumping into the lake to get wet and then standing on shore with a bar of ivory soap to lather up and then jumping back into the lake to get all the soap off. I have to say that I didn't do that too often. Besides polluting the lake I couldn't do it if my daughters were around. Tom and Bill had a much better plan. After supper when it starts getting dark, and if the mosquitoes aren't too bad, you heat up a pot of water and then add some of that to cold water to make warm water and then add the rest to another pot to make hot water. Then you go to the edge of the camp out of everyone's sight, strip off you clothes and pour the bucket of warm water on your self followed by soaping yourself down. Then you take the pot of hot water which has cooled down some and pour that over yourself to rinse off all the soap. It works great and you feel much better afterwords.

That's about all I can say except wear your life jackets and use common sense when you're on your trip. God gave us this beautiful wilderness not only to enjoy but also to protect and care for like a precious jewel.

END

John C. Dailey is a graduate of the University of Notre Dame and the University of Illinois College of Medicine. After serving two years in the Navy, he completed a Residency in Otolaryngology at the University of Wisconsin. He lives in Jacksonville, Illinois.

www.ingramcontent.com/pod-product-compliance
Lightning Source LLC
Chambersburg PA
CBHW060538010526
44119CB00052B/749